BEST OF

Tallinn

Regis St Louis

D1253262

How to use this book

Colour-Coding & Maps

Each chapter has a colour code along the banner at the top of the page which is also used for text and symbols on maps (eg all venues reviewed in the Highlights chapter are orange on the maps). The fold-out maps inside the front and back covers are numbered from 1 to 5. All sights and venues in the text have map references; eg, (3, B3) means Map 3, grid reference B3. See p64 for map symbols.

Prices

Multiple prices listed with reviews (eg 10/5kr) usually indicate adult/concession admission to a venue. Concession prices can include senior, student, member or coupon discounts. Meal cost and room rate categories are listed at the start of the Eating and Sleeping chapters, respectively.

Text Symbols

- ☎ telephone
- ✉ address
- 🖳 email/website address
- € admission
- ☺ opening hours
- ⓘ information
- Ⓜ metro
- 🚍 bus
- Ⓟ parking available
- ♿ wheelchair access
- ✖ on-site/nearby eatery
- 👶 child-friendly venue
- Ⓥ good vegetarian selection

Best of Tallinn
1st edition – Jun 2006

Published by Lonely Planet Publications Pty Ltd
ABN 36 005 607 983

Australia Head Office, Locked Bag 1, Footscray, Vic 3011
    ☎ 03 8379 8000 fax 03 8379 8111
    🖳 talk2us@lonelyplanet.com.au
USA 150 Linden St, Oakland, CA 94607
    ☎ 510 893 8555 toll free 800 275 8555
    fax 510 893 8572
    🖳 info@lonelyplanet.com
UK 72–82 Rosebery Avenue, London EC1R 4RW
    ☎ 020 7841 9000 fax 020 7841 9001
    🖳 go@lonelyplanet.co.uk

This title was commissioned in Lonely Planet's London office by Fiona Buchan and produced by Cambridge Publishing Management Limited. **Thanks** to Glenn Beanland, David Burnett, Steven Cann, Piotr Czajkowski, Brendan Dempsey, Ryan Evans, Quentin Frayne, Joshua Geoghegan, Michala Green, Mark Griffiths, Imogen Hall, Glenn van der Knijff, Anthony Phelan, Charles Rawlings-Way, Michael Ruff, Wibowo Rusli, Fiona Siseman, Ray Thomson, Rachel Wood

Photographs by Lonely Planet Images and Jonathan Smith except for the following: p22 allOver photography/Alamy, p23 Hannu Liivaar/www.shutterstock.com

Cover photograph Robert Mullen/Alamy, The view from Raeapteek, the old pharmacy building on Raekoja plats.

All images are copyright of the photographers unless otherwise indicated. Many of the images in this guide are available for licensing from Lonely Planet Images: www.lonelyplanetimages.com.

ISBN 1 74104 750 1

Printed through Colorcraft Ltd, Hong Kong.
Printed in China

Contents

From the Publisher

THE AUTHOR
Regis St Louis

Regis, a Slavic languages and literature graduate of Indiana University, first came under Tallinn's spell during his student days at Moscow University, when Estonia was still referred to as a wayward state rather than an autonomous nation. Since then, he's avidly followed developments in the medieval capital as it's gone from ex-Soviet to EU, becoming one of Europe's rising stars along the way. Tallinn's baroque skyline, its haunted wine cellars and vibrant but quirky pop culture (sprat tins and intoxicating Vana Tallinn notwithstanding) are several reasons why he can't stop daydreaming about his next return. Regis is also the author of the Estonia chapter for the Lonely Planet *Estonia, Latvia & Lithuania* guide. He lives six blocks from *Eesti Maja* (the Estonian House) in New York City.

Many thanks to Fiona Buchan for inviting me on board. In Tallinn, I'm deeply grateful to Steve Kokker for the warm welcome and many kind introductions. I also thank Kaarel and Kadri, Alar, Anton and Tõnnu for their hospitality and insider tips. Big thanks to Cassandra, my intrepid travelling partner.

LONELY PLANET AUTHORS

Why is our travel information the best in the world? It's simple: our authors are independent, dedicated travellers. They don't research using just the Internet or phone, and they don't take freebies in exchange for positive coverage. They travel widely, to all the popular spots and off the beaten track. They personally visit thousands of hotels, restaurants, cafés, bars, galleries, palaces, museums and more – and they take pride in getting all the details right, and telling it how it is. For more, see the authors section on **www.lonelyplanet.com**.

PHOTOGRAPHER
Jonathan Smith

Raised in rural Aberdeenshire, Jon graduated from Scotland's St Andrews University in 1994 with an MA Honours in German and little idea of what to do with his life. After a spell teaching languages in newly independent Lithuania, he spent three years travelling around the former USSR, trying to carve himself a niche as a freelance travel photographer.

Jon's byline has appeared in over 100 Lonely Planet titles and recent commissions have included Lonely Planet's *Paris*, *St Petersburg* and *Moscow* city guides. An Eastern European specialist, Jon has a particular soft spot for Tallinn, the city where he had his first big break as a pro. He says the highlights this time were watching the sunset from Pirita beach, nibbling on Olde Hansa's roasted almonds and jiving with the bunnies at an animal themed disco in Club Hollywood.

SEND US YOUR FEEDBACK

We love to hear from travellers – your comments keep us on our toes and help make our books better. Our well-travelled team reads every word on what you loved or loathed about this book. Although we cannot reply individually to postal submissions, we always guarantee that your feedback goes straight to the appropriate authors, in time for the next edition – and the most useful submissions are rewarded with a free book. To send us your updates – and find out about Lonely Planet events, newsletters and travel news – visit our award-winning website: **www.lonelyplanet.com/feedback**.

Note: We may edit, reproduce and incorporate your comments in Lonely Planet products such as guidebooks, websites and digital products, so let us know if you don't want your comments reproduced or your name acknowledged. For a copy of our privacy policy visit **www.lonelyplanet.com/privacy**.

Introducing Tallinn

Perched on the edge of the Baltic Sea, Tallinn is an enchanting city whose history dates back many centuries. The medieval silhouette of Old Town, Tallinn's jewel, rises up just blocks from the bay, and is a bewitching image to those arriving by sea. This World Heritage-listed site contains a warren of narrow cobbled streets skirting beneath the spires of 13th-century churches and looming fortress walls. While proud of its rich past – this was, after all, where Europe's tallest building stood in the 14th century – Tallinn is also Estonia's economic and cultural capital, an embracer of all things technological and an active participant in the EU.

A casual exploration of Tallinn is a revelation of these splendid contrasts. You can spend the afternoon gazing at baroque masterpieces, then soak up the electronic music scene at a stylish lounge; or visit Old Town's many colourful boutiques followed by an evening stroll along the waterfront.

Tallinn's café culture is hard to match. Cosy, candlelit anterooms, art deco patisseries and breezy sunlit patios are the settings for strong coffee and people-watching, a fine prelude to the city's alluring restaurants and bars. Charming wine cellars, decadent old-world dining rooms and enticing bistros provide the backdrop to exquisite dishes from every savoury corner of the globe.

Tip-top roof detail at the Linnateater (p40)

Those in search of the traditional can find it at the much vaunted Estonian sauna, or wander through Peter the Great's former palace inside Kadriorg Park. Nearby, there are coastal islands, sandy beaches, even a bizarre cliff-top military base right out of a sci-fi film.

The city of Tallinn has had many masters over the years, which may be one reason why it has such a resilient, adaptable population. Regardless, since regaining its independence from Russia in 1991, Tallinn has reopened its doors to the world, and there's never been a better time to discover one of Europe's most charming medieval capitals.

Neighbourhoods

Tallinn's heart is its **Old Town**, a labyrinthine area of old cobblestone streets, lined with houses dating back to the Middle Ages. Here, you'll find the city's best galleries and museums, medieval churches and a colourful assortment of cafés, restaurants and bars. Old Town (Vanalinn) divides neatly into **Upper Town** and **Lower Town**. Upper Town on **Toompea** (the hill dominating Tallinn), with its splendid views, was the medieval seat of power. It still contains the parliament buildings. Lower Town spreads around the eastern foot of Toompea, and a 2.5km defensive wall still encircles much of it. The centre of Lower Town is **Raekoja plats**, a large square lined with restaurants and cafés (alfresco in summer).

Old Town's northern edge lies just a few hundred metres from **Tallinn Bay** (Tallinna Laht), which forms the southern shore of the Gulf of Finland. Around Old Town is a belt of green parks that follow the line of the city's original moat defences. Radiating out from this old core is **New Town**, dating from the 19th and early 20th centuries. **Vabaduse väljak** (Freedom Square) is today's city centre on the southern edge of Old Town.

East of Old Town, you'll find **Kadriorg Park**, an extensive green area with several museums and a tiny pond full of swans. Its neighbouring streets are lined with old wooden houses and plenty of trees, making an idyllic setting for a stroll. Further east is **Pirita Beach**, a small sandy stretch that attracts Tallinn's younger set in the summer. Nearby is the Pirita River, where it's possible to hire rowing boats for a leisurely trip along the peaceful river. Still heading eastward, you'll reach the **Botanical Gardens** and the **TV Tower**, a monument to Soviet power of the late 1970s.

West of Old Town, you'll find the small **Tallinn Zoo** and the more impressive **Open Air Museum**, where some of Estonia's oldest wooden buildings are preserved.

OFF THE BEATEN TRACK

Tallinn gets very busy in the summer months. To escape the throngs of tourists jamming Old Town's narrow streets, head to leafy Kadriorg Park (p13) for a stroll through greenery en route to Peter the Great's baroque palace. There's plenty of room in the park to walk, cycle or picnic. Even greener pastures can be found at the Botanical Gardens (pp18-19).

Those in search of the genuine Baltic beach experience should head up to Pirita Beach (p19), the local residents' favourite. A quieter sea-side experience can be had at Pelguranna Beach (p19), just a few kilometres west of Old Town.

Itineraries

Most of Tallinn's attractions are located in Old Town, making for easy exploration on foot. If you have limited time, you might consider the Tallinn Card (www.tallinn.ee/tallinncard), which gives free entry to many sights, free use of public transport, and shopping discounts. One-/two-/three-day cards cost 350/400/450kr (125/150/175kr for children) and include a 2½-hour city tour. Purchase cards at tourist information centres, hotels and travel agencies.

DAY ONE

Start your day with pastries and coffee at atmospheric **Kehrwieder** (p34) before hitting the **City Museum** (p9). Grab lunch at **Pegasus** (p32) then wander through Upper Town, where handicrafts shops abound. Bring your camera for snapshots at the **Danish King's Courtyard** (p19). That night treat yourself to dinner at **Olde Hansa** (p31).

DAY TWO

On your second day, visit **Kadriorg Park** (p13) and stroll through its neighbouring streets, stopping in **Villa Thai** (p33) for lunch. Back in Old Town, get your caffeine fix at **Café Chocolaterie** (p34) before dining at **Le Bonaparte** (p31).

DAY THREE

It's time to pick up the pace. On your third day, **rent a rowing boat on Pirita river** (p20), go for a run along scenic **Pirita Tee** (p19) or take a swim out at **Pirita Beach** (p19). Follow your workout with a relaxing **sauna** (p54). As the afternoon wanes, catch the sunset over the city from the monumental **TV Tower** (p18). More great views await at the classic wine bar **Vinoteek** (p38), a good spot to start off the night. Have dinner at nearby **Õ** (p31), followed by a cocktail at **Spirit** (p35). If it's your last day in town, don't call it a night before hitting one of the clubs. For an excellent dance crowd, make your way to **Club Hollywood** (p39).

Elegant spires in Old Town

Highlights

RAEKOJA PLATS (4, C3)

Tallinn's Town Hall Square has been the centre of civic life since markets began here in the 11th century (the last was in 1896). Today, it's a vibrant place ringed with cafés and restaurants, and during the summer the square becomes the backdrop to Tallinn's liveliest street scene. Rising over the plats is the **Town Hall** (Raekoda), one of Estonia's most iconic buildings and the only surviving Gothic town hall in northern Europe. It was built between 1371 and 1404, and was the seat of power in the medieval Lower Town. According to legend, its minaret-like tower was modelled on a sketch made by an explorer following his visit to the Orient. Tallinn's symbol – the pike-bearing guardsman named Vana Toomas (Old Thomas) – stands atop the tower. He serves double duty as a weather vane – a post he's held since 1530 – though this is his third incarnation, having been destroyed by fire several times over the last few centuries. The gargoyles in the form of dragons' heads were added in the 17th century. The teeming market from the Middle Ages was held beneath the ground-level arches on the north side.

Inside the Town Hall is the **Citizens' Hall**, with an impressive vaulted roof and fine 1374 bench-ends that are among Estonia's oldest wooden carvings. The adjoining tower, reaching 64m at the tip of the spire, offers fine views over the town, but it's only open in the summer. Saturday concerts are often held in the Citizens' Hall. During the summer months the cellar below hosts exhibitions (usually some variation on a Hanseatic theme).

INFORMATION
- ☎ 645 7900
- 🖳 www.tallinn.ee/raekoda
- ✉ Raekoja plats
- € Tower 25/15kr; Citizen's Hall 35/20kr
- ☾ Tower 11am-6pm Tue-Sun Jun-Aug; Citizen's Hall 10am-4pm Tue-Sun Jul-Aug & by appt Sep-Jun
- ✖ Tristan ja Isolde (p35)

The Raeapteek is an ancient Tallinn institution

DON'T MISS

The Raeapteek (Town Council Pharmacy), on the northern side of the square, is one of the world's oldest pharmacies that is still in use. The building has served as a pharmacy or apothecary since at least 1422, once passing through 10 generations of the same family. Its present façade dates from the 17th century.

CITY MUSEUM (4, D3)

A few blocks north of Raekoja plats, the three-storey City Museum (Linnamuuseum) traces the city's development from its earliest days up to the present. Set in a medieval merchant's house, the museum has interactive exhibits that portray what life was like for the average Tallinn citizen throughout the last 700 years (though the focus is more on the upper classes in the earlier centuries). Displays of clothing, tapestries, furnishings, and church and guild relics, all with English signage, assist in the time travel. Of particular note is the documentation on the population explosion experienced during the late 19th century, when industrial growth was fuelled in part by the completion in 1870 of the railway that connected Tallinn with St Petersburg. The third floor presents a politicised (but quite accurate we imagine) portrait of life under the Soviet yoke, complete with WWII photos, propaganda posters and plenty of USSR memorabilia. There's also a fascinating video of the events surrounding the collapse of the regime in 1991.

In addition to permanent displays, curators host temporary shows, and you never know what's in store – on a recent visit, we caught a baffling exhibition on the evolution of women's undergarments over the last 75 years.

Open the door to the City Museum's fascinating displays of Tallinn life

INFORMATION

- ☎ 644 6553
- 🖳 www.linnamuuseum.ee (in Estonian)
- ✉ Vene tänav 17
- € 35/10kr
- 🕙 10.30am-6pm Wed-Mon Mar-Oct, 10.30am-5pm Wed-Mon Nov-Feb
- ✗ Elevant (p30)

TALLINN'S FOREIGN RULERS

Throughout Tallinn's history, the great regional powers battled for the city's control, with German Knights, Danes, Swedes, Poles and Russians all entering the fray. Although Russia dominated the longest (1710–1918 and 1940–91), many consider the Swedish period in the 17th century to be the city's most peaceful and prosperous.

ST NICHOLAS CHURCH (4, C4)

Southwest of the main square stands the Gothic St Nicholas Church (Niguliste Kirik), yet another of Tallinn's medieval treasures. Originally dating from the 13th century, St Nicholas was expanded and redesigned over the next four centuries.

DON'T MISS

At the foot of the slope below St Nicholas Church, along Harju tänav, you can see more ruin wrought by Soviet bombers on the night of 9 March 1944. A sign in English facing Harju tänav details the damage inflicted on the city that night.

Today St Nicholas houses artwork from other medieval Estonian churches. Its most famous work is a wall-sized fragment from an eerie *Danse Macabre*, a 15th-century masterpiece painted by the German artist Berndt Notke. No one knows how this portrayal of a skeleton leading the living to the grave made its way from Lübeck to Tallinn, but it is believed to be the only surviving *Danse Macabre* painted on canvas that has survived up to the present. Other artefacts here include Renaissance and baroque chandeliers; a 15th-century altar that once belonged to the Blackheads guild (p16); and a silver chamber, with shimmering works from Tallinn's old silversmiths' guild. Over the altarpiece stretches a large painting of the life of St Nicholas, completed in the 15th century by Hermen Rode, another Lübeck artist.

The church was badly damaged by Soviet bombers in 1944 and by a fire in the 1980s, but today stands fully restored. The acoustics are first-rate, with organ recitals held here most weekends (beginning at 4pm on Saturday and Sunday).

St Nicholas Church is a treasure trove of medieval Estonian art

INFORMATION

☎ 644 9903
🖳 www.ekm.ee
✉ Niguliste tänav 3
€ 35/20kr
🕑 10am-5pm Wed-Sun
🍽 Pegasus (p32)

DOME CHURCH (4, B4)

Estonia's oldest church, Dome Church (Toomkirik) was founded in the early 13th century by the earliest Danish conquerors of the region. It stands on Toompea hill which, with its fine views over the town and harbour, became the birthplace of Tallinn when the German Knights of the Sword built a fortress here around 1230. Incidentally, the hill is also sacred to native Estonians, who consider it the legendary burial mound of Kalev, the heroic first leader of the Estonians. Although the site of the church was first consecrated in 1240, the edifice of this magnificent Lutheran cathedral church dates from the 15th and 17th centuries, with the tower added in 1779. Among other things, the church was once a burial ground for the rich and noble. The finest of the carved tombs inside are those on the right as you approach the altar, including life-size figures of the 16th-century Swedish commander Pontus de la Gardie and his wife. The Swedish siege of Narva, where de la Gardie died, is shown on the side of the sarcophagus. The marble Greek temple-style sarcophagus belongs to Admiral Samuel Greigh, an 18th-century Scot who joined the Russian navy and became a hero of Russo-Turkish sea battles. The inscription contains words of regret that Catherine II expressed at his death. Admiral Adam Johann von Krusenstern, a German Estonian who was the first Russian citizen to sail around the world in 1803, also has an elaborate tomb.

INFORMATION

- ☎ 644 4140
- ✉ Toomkooli tänav 6
- € free
- 🕥 9am-4pm Tue-Sun
- 🍴 Bogapott (p34)

DON'T MISS

The city's favourite lookout over Lower Town lies just a few steps away. From Dome Church, follow Kohtu tänav north until you reach the panoramic view (4, C3).

The great and the good of Tallinn are buried in the Dome Church

MUSEUM OF OCCUPATION & FIGHT FOR FREEDOM (4, B5)

One of Estonia's newest attractions, this museum opened to much critical acclaim (and some criticism) in 2003. Visitors will get a sense of the harsh repression that Estonians experienced during five decades that began with WWII. After Nazi tanks rolled across the border, the suffering began. One thousand Estonian Jews were executed, and some 20,000 Jews from other countries were sent into the country to die here. The more lasting memory of suffering is that period under Soviet rule, from 1944 until 're-independence' in 1991. The walls of one room are lined with old suitcases, symbolising some 100,000 Estonians who fled the country. A

INFORMATION

☎ 668 0250
🖥 www.okupatsioon.ee
✉ Toompea tänav 8
€ 10/5kr
🕙 11am-6pm Tue-Sun

simple wooden boat used by some escapees is also on display. Exhibitions show what life was like in the gulags (through displays like the flimsy clothing prisoners wore during the Siberian winters) and what might land a person there (a few typed pages of anti-Soviet literature that was passed between readers). Photos of some of those who were sent there (over 35,000 men, women and children) are particularly moving. The museum also contains film footage of some of the brutalities of the time.

Some critics thought the museum's treatment of the USSR was too harsh – particularly in placing images like the swastika and the red star side by side. Those who suffered through the era or fled – as was the case with the museum's founder – believe otherwise.

Strike a light: Soviet-era matchboxes

THROUGH SUFFERING, HOPE

At the inauguration of the museum, Olga Ritso and then-prime minister Juhan Parts formally opened the new museum by cutting not a ribbon but a strand of barbed wire. Ritso had been a fortunate survivor (having fled by boat following the Soviet-ordered deaths of her father and uncle) and now in her 80s was seeing one of her dreams come to fruition: a concrete memorial to those who lived (and died) under Nazi and Soviet rule. Ritso and her husband's US$2 million donation to create the museum ranks among the largest private donations in Estonia's history.

KADRIORG PARK (2, B2)

INFORMATION

Kadriorg Palace & Museum of Foreign Art

☎ 606 6400

🖥 www.ekm.ee

✉ Weizenbergi 37

€ 45/20kr

🕐 10am-5pm Tue-Sun May-Sep,
10am-5pm Wed-Sun Oct-Apr

🚊 1, 3 to Kadriorg stop

🍴 Cantina Carramba (p30)

This pleasant, wooded area lies 2km east of Old Town, and remains a long-time favourite of city dwellers seeking a bit of green space. Oak, lilac and horse chestnut trees are the setting for strollers, cyclists and picnickers, and the park's ample acreage means that the paths never feel crowded. Together with the baroque Kadriorg Palace, it was designed in the 18th century by the Italian Niccolo Michetti for the Russian tsar, Peter the Great, soon after Peter's conquest of Estonia in the Great Northern War.

The centrepiece of the forest is the **Kadriorg Palace & Museum of Foreign Art**, built between 1718 and 1736 – with the help of Peter himself, who laid no fewer than three sturdy bricks. (Incidentally, these were left bare to dazzle visitors.) The museum currently houses Dutch, German and Italian paintings of the 16th to the 18th centuries, along with Russian works from the 18th to 19th centuries. It's a nostalgic place to stroll for an hour or two among the mostly Romantic works, and there's a handsomely manicured flower garden at the back. In the 1930s, the palace was the private domain of the president of the independent Estonia. Since Estonia's re-independence, part of the palace complex has again become the presidential home.

Included in the admission price is a visit to the small **Mikkel Museum** with a limited but interesting assortment of art: Russian and Chinese paintings, 15th-century icons and works in porcelain.

Also in Kadriorg is the futuristic **Art Museum of Estonia**, a massive, seven-storey building that will house some 60,000 works by Estonian and foreign artists. Following its scheduled opening in early 2006, its 5000 square metres of exhibition space will contain the largest art collection in the Baltics.

DON'T MISS

Nearby is the cottage Peter the Great occupied on visits to Tallinn while Kadriorg Palace was under construction. Today it houses the **Peter the Great House Museum** (15kr; 11am-4pm Wed-Sat May-Sep) where you may examine his clothes and the boots he made. There's also a small collection of 18th-century furnishings.

They'll never find me… lose the kids for a bit at Kadriorg Park

OPEN AIR MUSEUM (3, OFF A3)

Back to the land: traditional Estonian architecture at the Open Air Museum

Set on the Bay of Kopli a few kilometres west of Old Town, Tallinn's Open Air Museum contains some of Estonia's oldest wooden structures. A wander through the 80-hectare area is like a stroll back in time when Estonia was still a largely rural place with customs and traditions linked deeply to the soil. Some 72 buildings make up this elaborate and carefully reconstructed village, complete with traditional farmhouses, several mills, an inn, a schoolhouse, a windmill, a fire station and a church dating from the late 17th century. If you're not heading to villages in the south, this is a good place to see traditional wooden architecture and get a real taste of rural life. To make the most of your time here, take advantage of the information-packed audio tour (80kr).

In addition to the rewards of learning about Estonian home-design traditions that date back to the Stone Age, visitors can also enjoy some excellent country cooking at the on-site Kolu Inn, which serves traditional Estonian meals. There are also views back to the city and some fine paths for walking through the woods or down to the sea. On Sunday mornings there are folk song and dance shows. If you have children in tow, don't overlook the pony rides.

INFORMATION
- ☎ 654 9100
- 🖥 www.evm.ee
- ✉ Vabaõhumuuseumi tee 12
- € May-Sep 30/15kr, Oct-Apr 15/10kr
- 🕑 buildings 10am-6pm; grounds 10am-8pm
- 🚌 21 or 22 to the zoo bus stop & a 15-minute walk along the seaside road
- ♿ fair
- 🍴 Kolu Inn (on site)

DON'T MISS
Lively festivals at the museum. The biggest is Jaanipäev or Midsummer Eve on 23 June, with music, revelry and a large bonfire. Another good time to visit is in December, when the museum transforms into a picturesque Christmas village.

Sights & Activities

CHURCHES & CATHEDRALS

Alexander Nevsky Cathedral (4, B4)

It is no accident that this impressive church, with its gilded domes, is centrally located opposite the parliament buildings: the church (built 1894–1900) was one of many Orthodox cathedrals built as part of a general Russification policy in the Baltic provinces in the late 19th century. Orthodox believers still come here in droves, and it's a beautiful church despite the politics.
☎ 644 3484 ✉ Lossi plats 10 € free ☼ 8am-7pm

Dominican Monastery (4, D3)

Founded in 1246, the Dominiiklaste klooster is one of Tallinn's oldest buildings. It once housed Scandinavian monks who aimed to convert Estonians to Christianity. The monastery was torched in 1524 by a mob of angry Lutherans in the grip of Reformation-era hysteria. Today it houses Estonia's largest collection of stone carvings, and the inner garden is a peaceful refuge from the summertime crowds.
☎ 644 4606 🖥 www. kloostri.ee ✉ Vene tänav 16

Echoes of Russia in the domes of Alexander Nevsky Cathedral

€ 45/25kr ☼ 9.30am-6pm mid-May–mid-Sep; visits other times by arrangement

Holy Spirit Church (4, D3)

Near Raekoja plats, this white 13th-century church boasts an impressive baroque tower and a wooden blue and gold clock that's much photographed by Tallinn's visitors. Fires have damaged the church repeatedly over the centuries, but the intricate wood-carved interior still remains.
☎ 644 1487 ✉ Pühavaimu 2 € 10kr ☼ 10am-3pm Mon-Fri ♿ fair

St Olaf Church (4, D2)

Rising at the northern end of Pikk is the majestic Oleviste Kirik, whose 124m spire is yet another of Tallinn's icons (and was used as a surveillance centre by the KGB). A superb view – Old

Town's best – awaits those who clamber up to the observation deck.
☎ 621 4421 🖥 www. oleviste.ee ✉ Pikk 48, entrance on Lai € 20/10kr ☼ 10am-6pm Jun-Aug

Sts Peter & Paul Catholic Church (4, D3)

This handsome whitewashed church was designed by Carlo Rossi, the famed architect who left his mark on the neoclassical shape of St Petersburg. Today Peeter-Paul Kirik still functions as Tallinn's only Catholic church – largely for the Polish and Lithuanian community.
☎ 644 6367 ✉ Vene tänav 16 € free ☼ 10am-6pm mid-May–mid-Sep; visits other times by arrangement

Ukrainian Greek-Catholic Church (4, D2)

This 14th-century wooden church is part of a small monastery and is full of old relics. Visits include a free guided tour, where you'll learn all about the history and legends of the place. Donations accepted (and go towards the recently opened school and cultural centre).
☎ 5668 2369 ✉ Laboratooriumi 22 € free ☼ 1-2.30pm Sun & by appt

---

MERCHANT HOUSES

For a window into the lives of the medieval gentry, take a stroll along Pikk tänav (meaning 'long street'), which runs north from Raekoja plats towards Tallinn port. There you'll find the houses of medieval German merchants and gentry. Many of these houses were built in the 15th century, of either three or four storeys, with the lower two used as living and reception quarters and the upper ones for storage.

GALLERIES

City Gallery (4, C5)
This small Old Town space hosts rapidly changing exhibits – often among the more noteworthy installations in the capital. ☎ 644 2818 ⌨ www. kunstihoone.ee ✉ Harju tänav 13 € free ⏱ noon-6pm Wed-Mon

Draakoni Gallery (4, C3)
This cosy Old Town space hosts small, sometimes stimulating, exhibitions. More than anything, though, we like this place for its fabulous sculpted façade. ☎ 646 4110 ✉ Pikk tänav 18 € free ⏱ 10am-6pm Mon-Fri, 10am-5pm Sat

Rotterman Salt Storage (4, F2)
East of Old Town, this beautifully restored limestone warehouse once served the unpoetic but utilitarian function as the city's salt cellar. Today, the massive space houses the permanent exhibitions of the Estonian Museum of Architecture. Less of a yawn is the incredible array of temporary exhibitions – often the city's best – held throughout the year. Check the website for details. ☎ 625 7000 ⌨ www. arhitektuurimuuseum.ee ✉ Ahtri tänav 2 € adult/ student 30/10kr ⏱ 11am-6pm Wed-Sun

Tallinn Art Hall (4, C5)
Daring, avant-garde Estonian art is on the menu at this imposing pre-Soviet-era building overlooking Freedom Square. After getting your fill of art, pop next door to stylish Moskva (p35) for a different brand of intoxicant. ☎ 644 2818 ⌨ www. kunstihoone.ee ✉ Vabaduse väljak 8 € 25kr ⏱ noon-6pm Wed-Sun

Vaal (3, E4)
This versatile exhibition space outside Old Town displays some of Estonia's best artists. For getting a grip on the contemporary scene, Vaal is a good place to start. ☎ 681 0871 ⌨ www.vaal.ee ✉ Tartu maantee 80D € free ⏱ noon-6pm Mon-Fri, noon-4pm Sat

MUSEUMS & GUILDS

Brotherhood of Blackheads (4, D3)
This guild building is the site of regular concerts – one nearly every evening in the summer. Blackheads were unmarried merchants who took their name not from poor hygiene, but from their patron saint, Mauritius, a legendary African warrior. His likeness is found between two lions on the building façade (dating from 1597). ☎ 631 3199 ⌨ www.mustpeademaja.ee ✉ Pikk tänav 24

Great Guild (4, C3)
Once the realm of only the most eminent merchants of Tallinn, the Great Guild is a striking building dating from 1410. Its vaulted halls now contain the State History Museum, with a rather dry permanent exhibition of Estonian historical artefacts

A graceful dragon guards the door at the Draakoni Gallery

Ouch! Anatomical model in the State History Museum at the Great Guild

dating from the 14th to the 19th centuries. Regular temporary shows often warrant the visit.
☎ 641 1630 ⬚ www.eam.ee ✉ Pikk tänav 17 € 15/10kr ⌚ 11am-6pm Thu-Tue

Maarjamäe Palace (3, F1)
This seldom-visited museum covers Estonian history from the mid-19th century onwards. The neo-Gothic limestone palace was built in the 1870s as a summer cottage for the Russian general, A Orlov-Davydov.
☎ 601 4535 ✉ Pirita tee 56 € 10/8kr ⌚ 11am-6pm Wed-Sun

Maritime Museum (4, D2)
Inside the stocky tower known as Fat Margaret (Paks Margareeta) lies the Maritime Museum, with displays of old charts, model ships, antiquated diving equipment and other relics from Estonia's seafaring history. There are good views from the platform on the roof.

☎ 641 1408 ✉ Pikk tänav 70 € 25/10kr ⌚ 10am-6pm Wed-Sun

St Canutus Guild Hall (4, D3)
Another old artisans guild on Pikk is the 1860 St Canutus Guild Hall, a photogenic building with its statues of Martin Luther and St Canute looking down from their second-storey perch. Inside, the hall functions as a performance space for modern dance.
☎ 646 4704 ⬚ www.saal.ee ✉ Pikk tänav 20

Tammsaare Museum (3, E3)
Just west of Kadriorg Park, the last home of the great Estonian novelist Anton Hansen Tammsaare now contains a small museum with period furnishings from the 1930s. The house lies on a tree-lined street among other charming 19th-century homes, and the whole neighbourhood makes a great setting for a stroll. Between the wars, this was Tallinn's most affluent area.

☎ 601 3232 ✉ Koidula tänav 12A € 5kr ⌚ 11am-6pm Wed-Mon

BUILDINGS & MONUMENTS

Broken Line (4, D1)
Outside the Great Coast Gate stretches two strands of a long sculpture entitled *Broken Line*, dedicated to those who perished when the *Estonia* ferry sank, Europe's worst peacetime maritime tragedy. Nearby, a 3m-long granite tablet lists the 852 people who died that night (28 September 1994) travelling from Stockholm to Tallinn.
✉ Pikk tänav/Rannamäe tee

Former KGB Building (4, D2)
Just south of St Olaf Church is the former KGB headquarters. The building's basement windows were bricked up to prevent the sounds of violent interrogations from being heard by those passing by on the street.
✉ Pikk tänav 46/48

Great Coast Gate (4, D1)

The medieval exit to Tallinn port lies just north of St Olaf Church. It's joined to Fat Margaret (Paks Margareeta), a rotund 16th-century bastion that protected this entrance to the town. Fat Margaret's walls are more than 4m thick at the base.

✉ Pikk tänav 70

Kiek-in-de-Kök (4, B4)

One of Tallinn's most formidable towers is the stout Kiek-in-de-Kök, which means 'Peep into the Kitchen' in Low German. This is exactly what bored soldiers did from their vantage point over Lower Town. The tower was built around 1475, and despite damage during the Livonian War, it never collapsed. Today it houses a museum tracing the early development of Tallinn.

☎ 644 6686
✉ Komandandi 2
€ 25/8kr ⌚ 10.30am-6pm Tue-Sun Mar-Oct, 10.30am-5pm Nov-Feb

Old Town Wall (4, C3)

The longest-standing stretch of the Old Town wall, with nine towers, spans the length of Laboratooriumi. To access the walkway atop the walls, go to the gate (and ticket office) at Suur-Kloostri and Väike-Kloostri tänav. Three empty towers are interconnected here and visitors can explore their nooks and crannies for themselves. There are good views from the tower windows.

✉ Laboratooriumi € 10/7kr ⌚ 11am-7pm Mon-Fri, 11am-4pm Sat & Sun

HAUNTED TALLINN

Near St Nicholas Church in front of Rataskaevu 16 is a well where many stray cats perished. In medieval times animals were sacrificed to appeal for prosperity in the year ahead. Some believe the house that stands near the well is haunted. The devil apparently hosted a wild party there some time ago, and if you happen to pass late one night, some say you can still hear unexplained sounds of the party.

Up on Toompea, a number of ghostly apparitions have been reported inside the Gate Tower (Lühike jalg 9), including a crucified monk and a black dog with burning eyes. It's thought to be the most haunted place in Tallinn.

Toompea Castle (4, B4)

At the top of Lühike jalg is this photogenic castle, which now houses the Riigikogu, Estonia's parliament. Nothing remains of the 1219 Danish castle, but three corner towers of its successor, founded by the Knights of the Sword in 1227–29, still stand. The pink baroque façade dates from the 18th century, when Catherine the Great had the castle rebuilt.

☎ 631 6537 ✉ Lossi plats 1 ⌚ visits by appt only 10am-4pm Mon-Fri

TV Tower (3, off F1)

For magnificent views over city and sea, it's hard to beat the 314m TV tower. On the ground floor are some colourful stained-glass Soviet-socialist artworks, while up at the 170m point, you'll find a Russian-style restaurant and panoramic viewing platform. At the base there are still a few bullet holes from events during the August 1991 attempted Soviet takeover.

☎ 623 8258
🖥 www.teletorn.ee

✉ Kloostrimetsa tee 58a
€ 50/15kr ⌚ 10am-midnight 🚌 34 & 38 (Motoklubi stop)

WWII Memorial (3, off F1)

Along Pirita tee is an unmistakably Soviet war monument, rising in its concrete glory to a sharp point. It was erected in 1975 over the graves of German soldiers who died fighting the Soviets on the Leningrad front. Today the monument has an air of desolation about it, and it's a fascinating relic from the old USSR.

✉ Pirita tee

PARKS & PUBLIC SPACES

Botanical Gardens (3, off F1)

Set in 123 hectares and surrounded by lush woodlands, the Botanical Gardens boast 8000 plant species scattered in a series of greenhouses and along a 4km nature trail. The gardens lie 2.5km east of Pirita.

☎ 606 2666
✉ Kloostrimetsa tee 52
€ 40/20kr ⏰ 11am-
4pm Tue-Sun 🚌 34 & 38
(Kloostrimetsa stop)

Danish King's Courtyard
(4, C4)
In Upper Town, this leafy
courtyard offers sweeping
views over Old Town. In the

A grim reminder: the WWII Memorial on Pirita Tee

summer, artists set up their
easels. One of the towers
here, the ironically named
Neitsitorn (Virgin's Tower;
Lühike jalg 9a), is said to
have been a prison for
medieval prostitutes.
✉ end of Lühike jalg

Hirvepark (4, B5)
This grassy park is a pleasant
downhill stroll from the Kiek-
in-de-Kök. In the summer
months, it's a casual meeting
spot for students and other
young Tallinn residents.
The grieving statue there
has come to symbolise the
tragic fate of those who were
deported from Estonia during
and after WWII.
✉ Falgi tee & Toompea
tänav

Pelguranna Beach
(3, off A3)
Some 4km due west of
the centre is this beach,
purported to be the cleanest
in the Tallinn area. It has a
distinctly local feel but is
a less crowded alternative
to Pirita.
🚌 40, 48 from Viru väljak

Pirita Beach (3, off F1)
The city's largest and most
popular beach lies just
6km east of the city centre.
Although it's no Bondi Beach,
Pirita is a quick getaway for
space-starved urbanites, and
there are plenty of young,
bronzed sun-lovers filling
the sands, with a handful of
laid-back cafés nearby.
🚌 1, 8, 34, 38

Pirita Tee (3, F1-2)
This coastal road curving
northwards alongside Tallinn
Bay makes an ideal walking
route. The sea view from
here is particularly striking
on summer nights, when
glowing sunsets light up
the sky late into the night.
It's also a popular stretch
for joggers, cyclists and
Rollerbladers.
🚌 1, 8, 34, 38

Pirita Yacht Club &
Olympic Sailing Centre
(3, off F1)
Near the mouth of the Pirita
River, this was the base for
the sailing events of the
1980 Moscow Olympics,
and international regattas
are still held here today. If
you're just passing through,
stop off at the Yacht Club,
a relaxing spot for a drink
alfresco. You can also hire
rowing boats nearby
(see p20).

SINGING FOR FREEDOM
Estonians have always been a singing people and, at
times, song has played more than just a secondary role
in civic life. In fact, the push towards independence
from the USSR gained tremendous momentum during
the Song Festivals of the late Soviet days. During the
1988 Song Festival, some 300,000 squeezed into the
Song Bowl, raising a public (and harmonic) cry for
independence. Some half a million came in 1990, the
last major festival before regaining nationhood. This
movement was later dubbed the 'Singing Revolution'.

You can visit the Song Bowl east of Old Town along
Narva maantee.

BOATING ON PIRITA RIVER

In summer **Pirita Boat Hire**, beside the road-bridge over the Pirita River, rents rowing boats and pedalos. It's an idyllic place for a leisurely float, with thick forest edging towards the water. There's also a pleasant café and restaurant nearby (Charital, p30).

☎ 621 2105 ✉ Kloostri tee 6a € rowing boats and pedalos from 75/50kr per hr ⏱ 10am-7pm mid-May-Sep

Convent of St Brigitta

(3, off F1)

The only fragment left from this early-15th-century convent is the Gothic gable. The rest was destroyed courtesy of Ivan the Terrible during the Livonian War in 1577. In 1996, Brigittine nuns in Estonia were granted the right to return to the convent and reactivate the monastery. The convent's completed new headquarters are adjacent to the ruins.

☎ 605 5000 ✉ Kloostri tee 8 € 20/10kr ⏱ 10am-6pm

QUIRKY TALLINN

Firefighting Museum

(4, E4)

Housed in Estonia's oldest surviving fire station, this five-room museum explains the history of firefighting in Estonia with displays of antiquated Soviet helmets and uniforms as well as water pumps and gruesome photos of charred bodies. There's even a clever doll's house that shows the 27 different ways you can accidentally burn your house down.

☎ 644 4251 ✉ www. rescue.ee ✉ Vana-Viru tänav 14 € 4kr ⏱ noon-5pm Tue-Sat

TALLINN FOR CHILDREN

If you're travelling with kids, Tallinn's Old Town — with its pretty medieval setting and lively street scene — is pure eye candy for the under-12 crowd.

Children's Gallery (4, C4)

This small gallery near Raekoja plats hosts workshops for children, and showcases the work of Estonia's youngest artists.

☎ 644 6873 ✉ Kuninga 6 € 6/3kr ⏱ 11am-6pm Wed-Mon

Puppet Theatre (4, C3)

This theatre has been keeping the animator's art alive since 1952. Performances are held on one of three stages — including the outdoor summer stage.

☎ 667 9555 ✉ www. nukuteater.ee ✉ Lai 1 € tickets 45-60kr ⏱ box office 10am-6pm

Tallinn Zoo (3, off A3)

This zoo houses one of the world's largest collections of wild goats — as well as 334 different species of mammals, birds, reptiles and fish. It's a good place for kid-mingling — the entire child population of northern Estonia is here on summer weekends.

☎ 694 3300 ✉ www. tallinnzoo.ee ✉ Paldiski maantee 145 € 50/20kr ⏱ 9am-7pm May-Aug, 9am-5pm Sep, Oct & Apr, 9am-3pm Nov-Mar ▣ 22, 6 from Vabaduse väljak

Tivoli (3, off A3)

Opposite the zoo, this small amusement park offers kids plenty of rides and food you'd rather they didn't eat.

☎ 656 0110 € day pass adult/child 175/120kr ⏱ noon-8pm Mon-Fri, 11am-8pm Sat-Sun, closed Oct-Apr ▣ 22, 6 from Vabaduse väljak

Kids ride in style at Tallinn Zoo

Trips & Tours

WALKING TOUR
Historic Highlights

Begin the tour in Raekoja plats. If the tower of the **Town Hall** (**1**; p8) is open, climb up for a fine view. Otherwise, walk east to Vene tänav, one of Tallinn's oldest streets. Visit the ruins of the **Dominican Monastery** (**2**; p15) then take the tiny alley Katariina käik, passing several handicrafts shops and a charming restaurant. On Müürivahe, walk south along the wall, stopping to admire the **Knit Market** (**3**; p27) before returning to Vene. Next, stop in the **City Museum** (**4**; p9), for the lowdown on Tallinn's 700-year history. Head west to Pikk tänav, passing the **Holy Spirit Church** (**5**; p15) and noting the

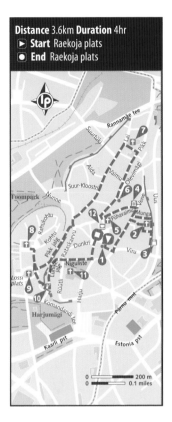

Distance 3.6km **Duration** 4hr
▶ **Start** Raekoja plats
● **End** Raekoja plats

guilds (**6**; pp16–17) before going to **St Olaf Church** (**7**; p15). Climb the tower for a superb view over Old Town. More views await as you head south to Pikk jalg and begin the ascent of Toompea. Stop in the **Dome Church** (**8**; p11) and **Alexander Nevsky Cathedral** (**9**; p15) before descending through the **Danish King's Courtyard** (**10**; p19). Go down the stairs along Lühike jalg, taking in more medieval highlights at **St Nicholas Church** (**11**; p10) before returning to Raekoja plats and a well-earned coffee at **Tristan ja Isolde** (**12**; p35).

Look up at the Great Guild Hall

DAY TRIPS
Island Escape

Who says you can't relive your favourite scenes from *The Blue Lagoon* in Nordic Estonia? Sure, it's no Bora Bora, but the country offers its share of lovely shoreline and remote island landscapes. Tallinn is an excellent gateway to the idyllic settings of Aegna and Naissaar islands.

AEGNA (5, D1)

Tiny Aegna, just 3 sq km, has been populated for centuries by fishermen and, from 1689, postal workers who operated mail boats from there to Sweden via Finland. During Soviet times it was an off-limits military base, but since the 1990s Tallinners have been building summerhouses there or just using the island for a quick escape into remote nature. There are some military remnants, an old church and cemetery, remains of a medieval village and long stretches of often deserted beaches.

> **INFORMATION**
> *12km north of Tallinn*
> 🏛 **MS Monika** (☎ 5657 7021
> 🖥 www.saartereisid.ee) runs two boats daily (three on Sundays) from Tallinn's Linnahall Terminal to Aegna (€ round trip to Aegna adult/student/bicycle 50/35/100kr, 1hr).
> ⌚ If you just come for the day you'll have eight hours on the island.

NAISSAAR (5, C1)

Naissaar, much larger than Aegna at 11km by 4km, has an even livelier history, thick forests and attractive coastline. Naissaar was once a bulwark for defending the capital. A railway was even built pre-WWI for speedier build-up of armaments. Curiously, in 1917–18, tsarist troops took the island and tried to form their own government. Soviet military traces remain, with an old army village, gun batteries and empty mines. There are dreamy stretches of unblemished beaches and two nature trails: south takes you past military ruins, a wooden church from 1856 and a cemetery for English sailors from the Crimean and Russo-Swedish wars; north leads through forests and mires and past erratic boulders. Just up the hill from the dock is the Nature Park Centre, where you can find lots of info, a warming coffee and a meal.

> **INFORMATION**
> *14km northwest of Tallinn*
> 🏛 **MS Monika** (☎ 5657 7021
> 🖥 www.saartereisid.ee) runs two boats daily on Saturdays and Sundays only. Boats depart from Tallinn's Linnahall Terminal to Naissaar (€ roundtrip to Naissaar adult/student/bicycle 180/120/200kr, 1hr).
> ⌚ If you're day-tripping, you'll have five hours on the island.

Eerie desolation: the abandoned Soviet military base at Paldiski

Paldiski (5, A3)

Hands down the most surreal place within a day's travel of Tallinn, Paldiski was once the most heavily militarised Soviet base along the Estonian coast. Today you'll find a vast network of crumbling old barracks, an eerie defunct nuclear submarine station, and a decaying town with a feeling of utter desolation. Not sold yet? Paldiski also has an appealing natural setting near some striking limestone cliffs overlooking the sea, as well as a bright red lighthouse – Estonia's tallest.

But cliffs and lighthouses aside, it's that weird Soviet past that draws most people here. You'll witness one of the grimmest legacies of the former occupiers.

This area was the first part of Estonia to be held by Soviet troops in 1939 and it was the last to see them leave in 1994. It became the main Soviet naval base in Estonia, and the town was a completely closed nuclear submarine station until 1994; only in 1995 were the decommissioned reactors

> ### INFORMATION
> *52km west of Tallinn*
> 🚆 From Tallinn's main train station (Balti jaam), 10 trains go daily to Paldiski (€ 16kr, 1¼hr)
> 🍴 Paldiski's only restaurant is Valge Laev (☎ 674 2095, Räe tänav 32), a nautically themed place on the main street in town.

removed. The reactors functioned continuously from the early 1970s until 1989. In 1994 a civilian died after stumbling upon radioactive materials – allegedly stolen from the disused base – on waste ground near Tallinn.

A trip to the lighthouse on the northwestern tip (follow the main road straight out of town) leads through destroyed army barracks and missile sheds. This is where some 16,000 soldiers were stationed. The former training sites are deteriorating but the odd bunker and a staircase built into the limestone, with markers showing strata of rock formation on the exposed sides of the cliff, are still visible.

ORGANISED TOURS

The tourist office (p57) and any travel agent can arrange tours with a private guide in English or other languages for around 235–315kr per hour. The city also offers several organised tours. Those seeking something a little different might opt for the bicycle tour.

Audioguide Old Town Walking Tour

On this self-guided tour, you follow a prescribed route through the medieval quarters, listening to historic details and anecdotes along the way. You can find the audio player at the tourist office (see p57) and at some hotels (see website for complete list).
🖳 www.audioguide.ee
€ 280kr

Bicycle Tour

This 14km bicycle tour covers Kadriorg Park, the Song Festival grounds, Pirita and Old Town, and includes commentary in English by the bicycle guide. The tour begins on Pirita tee, but staff can pick you up from Old Town. Book the day before. Price includes bike, helmet, and a very stylish green safety vest.
☎ 511 1819 🖳 www.citybike.ee ✉ Pirita tee 28
€ 220kr ⏰ 11am & 5pm Apr-Oct, 11am Nov-Mar

City Bus Tour

This red double-decker bus won't exactly help you blend in with the locals. It will, however, give you quick and easy access to a number of the city's top sights. The 48-hour bus pass allows you to hop on and off at the following stops, among others: Virju väljak, Toompea, Kadriorg, TV Tower, Botanical Gardens, Pirita. A recorded audio tour accompanies the ride (English, German, French, Spanish, etc). The tour straight through lasts $1^1/_2$ hours.
☎ 627 9080 🖳 www.citytour.ee € 320kr/free
⏰ 10am-4pm spring to autumn

Old Town Walking Tour

Offered in English or Finnish, this $1^1/_2$-hour tour covers Alexander Nevsky Cathedral, Dome Church, the viewing platform on Kohtu tänav and Lühike jalg and ends at Raekoja plats. Tours depart daily from the corner of Toompea and Komandandi.
☎ 610 8616
€ free with 24hr, 48hr or 72hr Tallinn Card; 100kr without card
⏰ 11:30am, 2pm, 4pm

Shopping

Old Town is packed with shops and boutiques selling Estonian-made handicrafts. You'll see leather-bound books, ceramics, jewellery, silverware, hand-blown glassware, objects carved out of limestone and traditional knitted sweaters, hats and gloves. You'll also find a plethora of antique shops selling Soviet memorabilia, old Russian icons and other fantastic curiosities you won't find at your local pound shop. In addition to that delicate bracelet and battered airman's jumpsuit, don't forget to bring back a bottle of Vana Tallinn.

HANDICRAFTS & ARTWORK

Bogapott (4, B4)
At this ceramics studio in Upper Town, you can watch potters in action as they skilfully shape vases, urns and decorative pieces on the wheel. Adjoining the studio space is a pleasant indoor-outdoor café.
☎ 631 3181 ✉ Pikk jalg 9 ☀ 10am-6pm

Domini Canes (4, D3)
Located in the highly atmospheric alley behind the Dominican Monastery, this lovely gallery-workshop keeps the ancient craft of glassmaking alive. Vases, glassware and lovely stained-glass works are for sale.
☎ 644 5286 ✉ Kateriina käik ☀ 11am-6pm

Katariina Gild (4, D3)
Next door to Domini Canes, this old merchant's house hides a row of handicraft stores and workshops. You'll find ceramics, leather-bound books, quilts, and loads more here.
☎ 641 8054 ✉ Kateriina käik ☀ 11am-6pm

Lühikese Jala Galerii (4, C4)
Located on the steps up to Toompea, this colourful, inviting gallery sells pure eye candy. In addition to some fantastic jewellery – some of which resembles exquisite works of art – you'll find ceramics, textiles and glassware.
☎ 631 3181 ✉ Lühike jalg 6 ☀ 10am-6pm Mon-Fri, 10am-5pm Sat-Sun

Madeli Käsitöö (4, D4)
This small but delightful shop features a unique selection of regional handicrafts – slippers from the island of Muhu, knitted dolls, hand-stitched tablecloths and the like.
☎ 620 9272 ✉ Väike-Karja 1 ☀ 10am-6pm Mon-Fri, 10am-4pm Sat-Sun

Navitrolla Galerii (4, B4)
One of Estonia's better-known artists, Navitrolla paints surreal landscapes peopled with dreamlike creatures and with titles like *Winged Sheep* and *Cat Licks His Balls*. His gallery on Toompea contains his signature oil paintings as well as his graphics found on T-shirts and coffee mugs.
☎ 631 3716 🖥 www.navitrolla.com ✉ Pikk jalg 7 ☀ 10am-6pm Mon-Fri, 10am-4pm Sat-Sun

ANTIQUES

Whether you're looking for that brass pocket watch with Uncle Joe's profile, the Lenin-head belt buckle or perhaps an old marching uniform, you'll find plenty of Soviet nostalgia buried in Tallinn's antique shops. There are tons of other gems waiting to be

Patches of vibrant colour at the Katariina Gild

unearthed (gramophones, furniture, silverware); you just have to dive in.

Antiik (4, D3)

One of the biggest antique stores in Old Town, Antiik has a particularly large selection of old icons (one of the best in the city), jewellery and curios. It's conveniently located on the northeast side of Raekoja plats.

☎ 631 4725
🖳 www.oldtimes.ee
✉ Raekoja plats 11
🕒 10am-6pm Mon-Fri, 10am-4pm Sat

Antiik & Kunst (4, C4)

Just a few steps from Raekoja plats, Antiik & Kunst has counters stocked with a good selection of the Soviet, the antique, and the downright baffling.

☎ 644 0923 ✉ Dunkri tänav 9 🕒 11am-6pm Mon-Sat

Antique, Military & Collections (4, C3)

As their unequivocal name suggests, these guys deliver the goods. This small two-room shop is one of the best places to load up on Soviet kitsch.

☎ 641 2606 ✉ Lai 4 🕒 10am-6pm

Reval Antiik (4, C5)

Candlesticks, pocket watches, Russian samovars and plenty of other 19th-century treasures lie hidden in this dusty shop near the south town wall.

☎ 644 0747
🖳 www.reval-antique.ee
✉ Harju 13, entrance on Müürivahe 🕒 10am-6pm Mon-Sat

VANA TALLINN & FRIENDS

The quintessential Estonian purchase, Vana Tallinn, is a liqueur that's sweet and strong with an aromatic scent and a pleasant after-taste. No one quite knows what's in the concoction that first emerged in the 1960s, but don't let that stop you from sampling the goods. It's best served in coffee, over ice with milk, over ice cream, or in champagne or dry white wine. If you need a quick fix, go ahead and chug it straight from the bottle. To sample more Estonian beverages, you might try Metsa Maasika, an unbearably sweet, strawberry-flavoured liqueur, or the egg-based Kiiu Torn, named after the smallest fortress in Estonia.

BOOKS & MUSIC

Allecto (4, D4)

This cosy bookshop has one of Tallinn's best selections of English-language books.

☎ 681 8731 ✉ Väike-Karja tänav 5 🕒 10am-7pm Mon-Fri, 10am-5pm Sat

Apollo (4, E4)

This handily located bookshop has loads of Lonely Planet books and other travel titles as well as foreign-language novels and periodicals, plus a comfy café on the second floor.

☎ 654 8485 ✉ Viru tänav 23 🕒 10am-8pm Mon-Fri, 10am-6pm Sat, 11am-4pm Sun

Dancemix (4, E6)

Focused on a wide variety of dance music, Tallinn's best record store is a rather modest affair, but it's a DJ favourite (vinyl available); and you'll find no better place to get the lowdown on who's who in the Baltic club scene.

✉ Kentmanni 19 🕒 12-8pm Mon-Fri, 12-6pm Sat

Soviet army memorabilia at Antique, Military & Collections

Stallholder at the Knit Market

Lõmatult Raamat (4, D4)
For used books in English and other languages, this place is a charming spot for a browse. Don't miss the random selection of vinyl records on the second floor.
☎ 683 7710 ⊠ Viru väljak 21 ⏲ 10am-7pm Mon-Fri, 10am-5pm Sat

Rahva Raamat (4, F4)
Another good reason to venture into the Viru Keskus mall (p28), Rahva Raamat sells guides, maps and English-language titles.
☎ 644 6655 ⊠ Viru Väljak 4 ⏲ 9am-8pm

MARKETS & SECOND-HAND SHOPS

Knit Market (4, D4)
Several blocks east of Raekoja plats, along the Old Town wall, there are a dozen or so vendors selling their handmade linens, scarves, sweaters and socks. Even if you don't plan to buy, it's an essential stop in Tallinn.
⊠ Müürivahe & Viru ⏲ 9am-5pm

Lai (4, C3)
Old Town's only second-hand shop, this funky place occasionally has some good finds – though you'll have to dig. If you collect records, don't overlook the back room.
☎ 641 1743 ⊠ Lai tänav 10 ⏲ 10am-8pm Mon-Sat

BOUTIQUES

Tallinn's designers have emerged from the post-independence lull and are slowly carving a niche for themselves among Europe's fashion scene. To see what's hot in the Estonian design

CLOTHING & SHOE SIZES

Women's Clothing

Aust/UK	8	10	12	14	16	18
Europe	36	38	40	42	44	46
Japan	5	7	9	11	13	15
USA	6	8	10	12	14	16

Women's Shoes

Aust/USA	5	6	7	8	9	10
Europe	35	36	37	38	39	40
France only	35	36	38	39	40	42
Japan	22	23	24	25	26	27
UK	3½	4½	5½	6½	7½	8½

Men's Clothing

Aust	92	96	100	104	108	112
Europe	46	48	50	52	54	56

Japan	S	M	M		L	
UK/USA	35	36	37	38	39	40

Men's Shirts (Collar Sizes)

Aust/Japan	38	39	40	41	42	43
Europe	38	39	40	41	42	43
UK/USA	15	15½	16	16½	17	17½

Men's Shoes

Aust/UK	7	8	9	10	11	12
Europe	41	42	43	44½	46	47
Japan	26	27	27.5	28	29	30
USA	7½	8½	9½	10½	11½	12½

Measurements approximate only; try before you buy.

BAYSIDE READING

Estonia has its share of celebrated writers, but unfortunately, they're little known abroad. One notable exception is Jaan Kross (b.1920), the literary lion from Tallinn whose incisive novels are informed in part by his own experiences in the Siberian gulag (1946–54). For an introduction to Kross, pick up *The Czar's Madman,* the tale of a 19th-century Estonian baron who falls in love with a peasant girl and later ends up in prison.

For a fascinating collection of photos and essays about Tallinn's subcultures, check out the bilingual *Tallinna Juht (A User's Guide to Tallinn)*, available in most bookshops.

world, visit the following stores – all near or inside Old Town.

Bastion (4, D4)

One of Estonia's most successful fashion houses, Bastion has a small but splashy women's collection, aimed at an older market.
☎ 644 1555 ✉ Viru tänav 12 ☯ 10am-7pm Mon-Fri, 11am-6pm Sat, 11am-4pm Sun

Hoochi Mama (4, F4)

Not just for halter-topped hotties from the Bronx, this colourful boutique has plenty of clubwear and other youthful fashions that run the gamut from the wild, the stylish to the indecent.
☎ 641 8866 ✉ Viru Keskus, Viru Väljak 4 ☯ 11am-8pm Mon-Thu, 11am-10pm Fri-Sat, noon-6pm Sun

Ivo Nikkolo (4, D4)

Stylish but staid, Ivo Nikkolo has neat, trim designs made with high-quality fabrics. Nikkolo is one of Estonia's most successful young designers.
☎ 644 4828 ✉ Suur-Karja 14 ☯ 10am-7pm Mon-Fri, 10am-5pm Sat, 10am-4pm Sun

Monton (4, F4)

Features a diverse collection of elegant, versatile designs. Like Ivo Nikkolo, Monton keeps things pretty classic, for women as well as men (the suits here are nicely cut). Inside the Viru Keskus shopping mall.
☎ 660 1847 ✉ Pärnu maantee 10 ☯ 9am-9pm

Nu Nordik (4, C5)

Unafraid of the avant-garde,

THE ONE-STOP SHOP

Tallinn's shiniest, newest mall, the **Viru Keskus** (4, F4), lies just outside Old Town. You'll find a wide selection of fashion choices here as well as a good bookshop (p27) stocking English-language titles, a grocery shop and plenty of eating options (including several open-air cafés on the west side).
☎ 610 1400 ✉ Viru Väljak 4 ☯ 9am-9pm

this small boutique has youthful, edgier designs, and it's a fun place to browse.
☎ 644 9392 ✉ Vabaduse väljak 8 ☯ 10am-6pm Mon-Fri, 11am-6pm Sat

FOOD & DRINK

Excelsior Vinoteek (4, C3)

This small modern wine shop is a handy place to pick up a bottle before picnicking or putting a dinner together.
☎ 631 3891 ✉ Rataskaevu tänav 2 ☯ noon-11pm Mon-Sat

Gloria Veinikelder (4, C4)

With a huge selection, this enormous wine cellar is an atmospheric place to browse for that perfect Shiraz to top the night off. Knowledgeable staff are on hand to match you with one of 2000 different wines and cognacs. If you feel like sampling the goods, head to the charming bar in the back.
☎ 644 6950 ✉ Müürivahe 2 ☯ 11am-11pm

Tallinna Kaubamaja (4, F4)

Located in the department store of the same name, this is one of the biggest grocery stores near Old Town. It's connected to the Viru Keskus shopping centre by a glass gallery.
✉ Gonsiori 2 ☯ 9am-10pm

Eating

Tallinn has an enormous variety of cuisine – from Estonian to Thai and with French, Italian, Indian and even Japanese options. Based in Old Town, the restaurant scene has a pretty unbeatable atmosphere: whether you want to dazzle a date or just soak up the medieval splendour alfresco, you'll find plenty of choices.

RESTAURANTS

African Kitchen (4, D2)
African €€
Authentic African cuisine, the upstairs patio is ideal for warm-weather days, while by night the lounge-like rooms inside make for a cosy retreat. Dishes feature flavourings of coconut, peanuts and red pepper, with a good selection of meat, seafood and vegetarian options.
☎ 644 2555 ⌨ www. africankitchen.ee ✉ Uus tänav 32 ☺ noon-midnight Ⓥ

Angel (4, D4)
International & Fusion €€
Exposed brickwork, rich wood tones and a trim lounge-like feel provide a warm setting for eating simple but tasty fare (salads, pastas – and an unbeatable cheeseburger). The late opening is perfect for those craving chicken curry in the early hours. Downstairs is Tallinn's best gay nightclub (p39).
☎ 641 6880 ✉ Sauna 1 ☺ noon-1am Sun-Tue, noon-4am Wed-Sat

Bakuu (4, C4)
Azerbaijani €€
Famed for their sizzling spits of *shashlyk* (shish kebab), this spartan Old Town restaurant delivers plenty of Azerbaijani favourites, including sampler platters for two. Grilled lamb and other meat dishes are on offer, as well as soups, salads, and fish (including mackerel *shashlyk*).
☎ 699 9680 ✉ Harju 7 ☺ 11am-11pm

Bocca (4, D2)
Italian €€€
Sophistication and style don't detract from the fresh, delectable cuisine served at this much-lauded restaurant. Creative dishes such as artichoke soup with grilled scallops and baked monkfish in creamy fennel sauce with black truffles match the strong wine list. Bocca also has a cosy lounge and bar, ideal for evening cocktails.
☎ 641 2610 ✉ Olevimägi 9 ☺ noon-midnight

African Kitchen: a taste of Africa in Estonia

Café VS (4, C6)
Indian €€
The velvet walls, coloured lights and profusion of polished metal may not be a setting you associate with chicken tikka masala, but in fact, this popular bar and late-night spot serves a tasty assortment of Indian cuisine. The crowd gets rowdier as the night progresses.
☎ 627 2627 ✉ Pärnu maantee 28 🕑 10am-midnight Mon-Thu, 10am-2am Fri, noon-2am Sat, noon-midnight Sun Ⓥ

Cantina Carramba (3, E3)
Tex-Mex €€
Boasting a delightful pueblo-esque colour scheme and a tasty selection of dishes, Cantina Carramba is ideally placed for a bit of indulgence after a walk in leafy Kadriorg Park. Burritos, fajitas and salads go down oh so nicely with the margaritas and Coronas.
☎ 601 3431
✉ Weizenbergi tänav 20a, Kadriorg 🕑 noon-11pm Mon-Sat, noon-8pm Sun

Charital (3, F1)
International & Fusion €€€
This lavishly set dining room boasts a superb setting along the Pirita River and a fairly crusty clientele. Traditional Euro fare is the norm here, but the lobsters are tops. Upstairs is a more laid-back café, a good stop-off after a morning's boating along the river (see p20).
☎ 623 7379 ✉ Kloostri tee 6 🕑 noon-11pm

Controvento (4, D3)
Italian €€
Hidden away on Tallinn's most atmospheric alleyway, this long-time favourite serves nicely prepared Italian dishes in a pleasant old-fashioned setting. In the summer grab a seat alfresco and let the time travel begin.
☎ 644 0470 ✉ Katariina käik 🕑 noon-11.30pm Ⓥ

Eesti Maja (4, E5)
Estonian €€
This fun folksy restaurant is a good place to sample authentic Estonian fare.

Traditional favourites like blood sausage, jellied pork and marinated eel aren't for the timid, but there are plenty of tasty dishes for the unadventurous (salmon, steak, etc). A small weekday lunch buffet is a good place to sample the goods.
☎ 645 5252 ✉ A. Lauteri tänav 1 🕑 11am-11pm 🚻

Egoist (4, D3)
French €€€€
Another of Tallinn's decadent places, Egoist has a small menu showcasing the classics of French haute cuisine: duck, lamb, wild trout, etc, served with panache in a 1600s-era building.
☎ 646 4052
✉ Vene tänav 33
🕑 noon-midnight

Elevant (4, D3)
Indian €€
Boasting a wide selection of vegetarian dishes and expertly prepared Indian cuisine, Elevant is an attractive spot for lingering over a meal. The winding wrought-iron staircase, airy furnishings and eclectic rhythms (bossa nova, progressive sitar) add to the charm.
☎ 631 3132
✉ Vene tänav 5
🕑 noon-11pm Ⓥ

Gloria (4, C4)
International & Fusion €€€€
Mick Jagger, Pope John Paul II and Jacques Chirac have all eaten here (though presumably they sat at different tables). What they enjoyed, you can, too: namely, a sumptuous pre-war dining room, professional service and

AROUND THE WORLD IN SEVEN MEALS
Locals will be the first to admit that traditional Estonian fare isn't for everyone (for more on that, see 'Acquired Tastes' p35). Pass on the blood sausages, and tempt yourself with some of the city's fine international cuisine. The following is a round-up of our favourite spots to indulge:
• Troika (p33) – Best Russian
• Le Bonaparte (p31) – Best French
• Villa Thai (p33) – Best Thai
• Must Lammas (p31) – Best Georgian
• African Kitchen (p29) – Best African
• Bocca (p29) – Best Italian
• Sushi House (p33) – Best Japanese

savoury dishes prepared with Estonian flare. The largest wine cellar in the Baltics is just downstairs.

☎ 644 6950 ✉ Müürivahe 2 ⏱ noon-midnight

Kapten Tenkeš (4, C6)
Hungarian €€

Just south of Old Town, this long-standing favourite serves up a variety of tasty Hungarian dishes in a pleasant, country-style setting. Picture dark wooden tables, enormous wreaths of garlic and an abundance of lacy decorations. The goulash and the Carpathian fish are among the top picks.

☎ 644 5630 ✉ Pärnu maantee 30 ⏱ noon-11pm Mon-Sat, 1-10pm Sun

Kompressor (4, C3)
Pancakes €

This popular student hangout is known for its inexpensive pancakes, which are delicious and filling. By night, the casual but colourful ambience makes this a nice detour for a drink.

☎ 646 4210
✉ Rataskaevu tänav 3
⏱ 11am-1am Mon-Thu, 11am-2am Fri-Sun ♿

Le Bonaparte (4, D2)
French €€€€

The emperor himself would've been hard-pressed to find fault with this venerable French restaurant. The delectable dishes match the impeccable service and the elegant dining room – making it not unsuitable for captious aristocrats, in other words. There's also an intimate wine cellar downstairs and a café in the foyer.

Top-notch French cuisine at Le Bonaparte

☎ 631 1755 ✉ Pikk 43 ⏱ noon-midnight

Mõõkkala (4, C4)
Seafood €€€€

Serving up some of the best seafood dishes in Estonia, Mõõkkala (which means 'swordfish') features an exquisite array of delicately prepared fish, including their excellent signature plate of grilled swordfish. The elegant décor, complete with deep blue walls and antique furnishings, makes a choice setting to impress a date.

☎ 641 8288 ✉ Kuninga 4 ⏱ noon-midnight

Must Lammas (4, D4)
Georgian €€

Preceded by a complimentary shot of house schnapps, meals at Must Lammas are a rewarding experience. Hearty, tasty plates of traditional fare wash down nicely with the Georgian wine. Try an entrée of *hatšapuri* (cheese bread) or

dolmas before delving into a sizzling kebab.

☎ 644 2031 ✉ Sauna tänav 2 ⏱ noon-11pm Mon-Sat, noon-6pm Sun

Ö (4, D2)
International & Fusion €€€

Named after a vowel that exists in few other languages, Ö has certainly carved a unique space in Tallinn's culinary world. The dining room, with its wild chandelier-sculptures, is an understated work of art – no less so than the fresh seafood, featuring inventive, Asian accents.

☎ 661 6150 ✉ Mere puiestee 6e ⏱ noon-midnight Mon-Sat, 1-10pm Sun

Olde Hansa (4, D4)
Medieval €€€

Amid candlelit rooms, with peasant-garbed servers shuffling between long wooden tables, Olde Hansa is the place to indulge in a sinfully gluttonous feast.

MENUS FROM THE MIDDLE AGES

While eating at a medieval-style restaurant may sound a little gimmicky, some say that you haven't really experienced Tallinn until you've dined at one of its 15th-century-modelled restaurants. At Olde Hansa (p31), the pick of the bunch, candles provide the only light as medieval-garbed servers hurry out of the shadows beneath enormous plates of roast meats and stews, the scent of mead and red wine tainting the air. The long wooden tables and festive air mean this is communal dining par excellence, with patrons indulging in the wide variety of authentically re-created dishes. Peppersack (see right) is another decent option for medieval fare.

If the roast meats, flagons of red wine and wandering minstrels sound a bit much, rest assured that chefs have done their part in producing historically authentic fare.
☎ 627 9020
✉ Vana Turg 1
🕑 11am-midnight 👶

Peetri Pizza (4, C5)
Pizza €€
This chain opened as soon as Estonia broke free from the USSR and was therefore practically synonymous with freedom. Pizzas are thin-crust and a bit on the flimsy side, though the outfit remains intensely popular with locals.

Also at Mere puiestee 6 (4, E3).
☎ 656 7567 (delivery)
✉ Pärnu maantee 22
🕑 11am-10pm 🅥 👶

Pegasus (4, C4)
International & Fusion €€€
In one of the most beautifully designed spaces in town, Pegasus serves eclectic fare with tasty seafood dishes, risottos, salads and grilled meats among the options. Breakfasts here are among Tallinn's best, while the upstairs lounge attracts Tallinn's better-dressed crowd.
☎ 631 4040 ✉ Harju 1
🕑 8am-1am Mon-Fri, 11am-2am Sat

Peppersack (4, D4)
Medieval €€€
Easily spotted by the sack of pepper dangling over the entrance, this restaurant serves grilled meat and hearty medieval fare. Sword fighting and nights of 'Oriental' dancing add an element of dinner theatre to the 15th-century setting.
☎ 646 6800
✉ Viru tänav 2 🕑 8am-midnight 👶

Pizza Americana (4, C4)
Pizza €€
Thick, tasty pizzas of every possible permutation are on offer here, including several vegetarian and seafood options. Red booths, blue walls and creamy white milkshakes will take you back to the land of Uncle Sam.
☎ 644 8837 ✉ Müürivahe 2
🕑 11.30am-10.30pm 🅥 👶

Sisalik (4, D3)
Mediterranean €€
Featuring a diverse Mediterranean menu and a handsome but understated interior, Sisalik is a welcome newcomer to the dining scene. Spanish tapas, grilled tuna and gnocchi with pesto and cherry tomatoes are among the selections.
☎ 646 6542 ✉ Pikk 30
🕑 noon-11pm Mon-Sat 🅥

St Michael Cheese Restaurant (4, C3)
International & Fusion €€€€
A cheese-lover's paradise, this warmly lit restaurant features cassock-wearing waiters serving plates of chateaubriand with feta; basil-and-cheese stuffed rockfish; and seafood wok

(for the non-cheese lovers) in a cosy restaurant set with medieval décor.
☎ 627 4845 ⊠ Nunne 14 ☾ 5pm-midnight

Sultan (4, D4)
Turkish €€
Tasty little platters of Turkish dishes (with Iberian accents) are the specialities at this airy restaurant. Lamb is the focus, though vegetarian options are available. Following the meal, retreat to the downstairs den for a bit of hookah (water-pipe) action.
☎ 644 4666
⊠ Väike-Karja 8
☾ noon-midnight Ⓥ

Sushi House (4, C4)
Japanese €€€
Combining 21st-century chic amid 14th-century ambience, Sushi House has style in spades. Among the top picks: tender fresh sushi and sashimi, yakitori (grilled meats) and some artfully arranged salads. Old wooden rafters, exposed brickwork and other medieval details add to the allure – as does its supposedly haunted past.
☎ 641 1900
⊠ Rataskaevu 16
☾ 11am-11pm

Texas Honky Tonk (4, D3)
Tex-Mex €€
Decked out like an old Texan saloon – complete with creaky wood floors and the smell of sawdust in the air – this lively restaurant is the best place in Old Town to load up on tacos, burritos, pork ribs and other dishes you wouldn't expect to find

this side of the Mason-Dixon Line. Kitschy ambience and a fun crowd.
☎ 631 1755 ⊠ Pikk 43 ☾ noon-midnight Sun-Thu, noon-2am Fri-Sat ♿

Troika (4, D3)
Russian €€
Tallinn's best Russian restaurant is a fully-fledged experience in itself, with wild hunting-themed murals, live accordion music, and an old-style country tavern upstairs. Even if you don't opt for delicious *pelmeni* (dumplings) or heavenly sweet borscht, stop in for an ice-cold glass of vodka.
☎ 627 6245 ⊠ Raekoja plats 15 ☾ noon-midnight

Vanaema Juures (4, C4)
Estonian €€
One of Tallinn's most stylish restaurants in the 1930s, this place still ranks as a top choice for Estonian fare. The antique-set dining room

is slightly formal, and the menu has plenty of options aside from the less-accessible fare such as pigs' trotters.
☎ 626 9080 ⊠ Rataskaevu tänav 12 ☾ noon-10pm Mon-Sat, noon-6pm Sun

Villa Thai (3, D3)
Thai €€
Villa Thai has a sublimely decorated interior: the use of bamboo, dark woods and richly coloured fabrics is in perfect harmony with the nicely prepared Thai and tandoori specialities.
☎ 641 9347 ⊠ Vilmsi 6 ☾ noon-11pm Ⓥ

CAFÉS
Forget Paris and Rome – Estonia's Old Town is so packed with cafés that you can spend your whole trip wandering wide-eyed and jittery from one charming, espresso-scented

Coffee and handmade chocolates at Café-Chocolaterie (p34) – what more could you ask for?

Café society on Raekoja plats (p8)

coffeehouse to the next. These cosy settings are fine spots to retreat to with a new friend on a chilly afternoon; or, if the setting inspires you, have a go at that murder mystery you've been aiming to write.

Bogapott (4, B4)

One of the only cafés in Upper Town, Bogapott serves coffee, pastries and fresh sandwiches amid plenty of medieval gloom. There's a pleasant courtyard in the front, as well as an art shop and an interesting ceramics studio next door.
☎ 631 3181 ✉ Pikk jalg 9 🕐 10am-6pm ♿

Café Anglais (4, D3)

A favourite with Tallinn's eccentrics and expats, this elegant café has a vaguely Parisian vibe and a delicious assortment of home-made cakes, coffees and light meals (try the warm salads). Despite the location, it

somehow eludes the tour-bussing masses.
☎ 644 2160 ✉ Raekoja plats 14 🕐 11am-11pm

Café Boulevard (4, F6)

Open all hours, this bright and cheery café/patisserie is the place of choice for insomniacs and late-night partiers. The ambience is late-Soviet, the crowd is hyped and the pies and cakes are pure decadence.
☎ 631 5891 ✉ Reval Hotel Olümpia, Liivalaia 33 🕐 24hr

Café-Chocolaterie (4, D4)

Nestled inside a tiny courtyard in Old Town, this inviting café seems like a hideaway at Grandmother's place. The antique-filled café also has delectable handmade chocolates – impossible to resist.
☎ 641 8061 ✉ Vene tänav 6 🕐 10am-11pm

Café Peterson (3, D3)

If you want a dash of culture with your style, head to

this charming café outside Old Town. A mix of local residents and students from neighbouring Tallinn Pedagogical University gather here. The café has an art gallery with colourful openings throughout the year, and there's live piano music some nights.
☎ 662 2195 ✉ Narva maantee 15 🕐 9am-11pm Mon-Sat, 10am-11pm Sun

Kehrwieder (4, C3)

This little cellar of a café is a perfect spot to stretch out on a couch, read by lamplight and bump your head on those old arched ceilings.
☎ 644 0818 ✉ Saiakang 1 🕐 11am-midnight ♿

Le Bonaparte (4, D2)

Flaky croissants, moist strawberry truffle cake, warm *pain au chocolat* – just a few of the reasons why Le Bonaparte ranks as Tallinn's best patisserie. The coffee and tea selections are also splendid – as is the medieval setting in which to enjoy it all. For more indulgence, try dining here (p31).

☎ 646 4444 ✉ Pikk tänav 45 ☺ 8am-10pm

Maiasmokk (4, C3)

Open since 1864, the city's oldest café still draws a crowd of greying admirers who appreciate the classic décor and pre-war feel. The pastries may taste like they were made on opening day, but who cares – the ambience is fantastic!

☎ 646 4066 ✉ Pikk tänav 16 ☺ 8am-7pm Mon-Sat, 10am-6pm Sun

Moskva (4, C5)

An attractive mix of Estonians, Russians and a few straggling out-of-towners gather at this très chic café and nightspot on the edge of Old Town. In addition to cocktails and cappuccino, Moskva serves blinis, salads and other light fare. The upstairs lounge is a slightly swankier place to imbibe – with DJs spinning to young crowds most weekends (cover charge around 75kr).

☎ 640 4694 🖳 www.moskva.ee ✉ Vabaduse väljak 10 ☺ 9am-midnight Mon-Thu, 9am-4am Fri, 11am-4am Sat, 11am-midnight Sun

Narva Kohvik (3, D3)

Time travel back to the days of Brezhnev at this unintentionally kitschy coffee house/restaurant outside Old Town. Serving up *stolovaya* (cafétería) favourites like wieners, borscht and *plov* (meat and vegetable pilaf), Narva Kohvik offers brusque

service, faded brown décor and a heavy dollop of unmitigated Soviet nostalgia. In short, it's the perfect place for brooding when life (or your entrée) has you down.

☎ 660 1786 ✉ Narva maantee 10 ☺ 10am-8pm Mon-Sat, 10am-6pm Sun

Spirit (4, E2)

This very inviting café and lounge is awash with rich textures – white stonework on the back wall, plush carpets, marble tabletops, a fire in the fireplace, and some poor creature's antlers on the wall. Like a page torn from a fashion mag, Spirit draws the young and fashionable who hold court here regularly.

☎ 661 5151 ✉ Mere puiestee 6e, entrance round the back ☺ noon-midnight Mon-Thu, noon-1am Fri-Sat, 1-10pm Sun

Tristan ja Isolde (4, C4)

A java-lovers' dream, this café built into the Town Hall features heavenly scents and a splendid medieval setting.

☎ 644 8759 ✉ Town Hall building, Raekoja plats ☺ 8am-11pm

Sweet treats: pastries at Le Bonaparte (p34)

Entertainment

Despite its compact size, Tallinn boasts plenty of distractions for the nightlife seeker – from candlelit wine cellars and stylish lounges to rowdy expat bars – and the capital's trim theatres and concert halls keep the arts going strong, all year long.

Buy tickets for concerts and mainstream events at Piletilevi (www. piletilevi.ee) and its central locations (there's one inside Viru Keskus, p28). Events are posted on city centre walls, advertised on flyers found in shops and cafés, and listed in newspapers. Several useful publications with listings are *Tallinn This Week* (www.ttw.ee) and *Tallinn In Your Pocket* (www. inyourpocket.com), both available at the Central Tourist Office (p57).

BARS

In addition to the places listed below, other stylish haunts include **Spirit** (p35), **Moskva** (p35), **Bocca** (p29) and **Pegasus** (p32).

Café VS (4, C6)
This quasi-industrial space serves a pretty mean tandoori chicken (see p30), but Café VS is better known for its lively bar, when locals and expats mix it up over brightly coloured cocktails. DJs spin an eclectic mix (house, Drum n Bass, R&B) Friday and Saturday nights.
☎ 627 2627
🖳 www.cafévs.ee
✉ Pärnu maantee 28
☯ 10am-midnight Mon-Thu, noon-2am Fri-Sat, noon-midnight Sun

Club Havana (4, C3)
A few locals and many tourists gather at this Latin-themed bar near Raekoja plats. At weekends, you'll find salsa dancing in the back room, bass-heavy music and a raucous, inebriated crowd.
☎ 640 6630 ✉ Pikk 11
☯ 10am-2am Sun-Thu, 10am-4am Fri-Sat

Depeche Mode (4, C3)
For fans of the '80s New Wave band, this may be the holy grail of drinking establishments. The bar is small and nondescript – aside from the DM played in heavy (some would say 'endless') rotation. Ask the owner about the time the Essex lads stopped in for a drink back in 2001.
☎ 644 2350 ✉ Nunne 4
☯ noon-4am

Gloria Veinikelder (4, C4)
This maze-like wine cellar and tapas restaurant has a number of nooks and crannies where you can secrete yourself with a date and/or a good bottle of Shiraz. The dark wood, antique furnishings and flickering candles add to the allure.
☎ 644 8846 ✉ Müürivahe 2 ☯ 11am-11pm

Hang out long enough at Depeche Mode and the boys from Basildon might just pop in for another drink

SPECIAL EVENTS

Estonia has a long list of festivals and cultural events, especially during the summer months. The Central Tourist Office in Tallinn (p57) has information on events around the capital. For a complete list of Tallinn's festivals, visit www.kultuur.info.

February

Student Jazz Festival (www.tudengijazz. ee) – This international festival held in mid-February attracts musicians from around the Baltic region.

April

Jazzkaar (☎ 611 4405; www.jazzkaar. ee) – Jazz greats from around the world converge on Tallinn during this excellent two-week festival. Don't miss it if you're in town.

Estonian Music Days (www.ehl.kul.ee) – This event in mid-April features both classical Estonian performances and new, emerging works.

June

Old Town Days – One of Tallinn's biggest annual events, this four-day fest held in early June features dancing, concerts, costumed performers and plenty of medieval merry-making on nearly every corner of Old Town.

Baltica International Folk Festival – A week of music, dance and displays focusing on Baltic and other folk traditions, this festival is shared between Rīga, Vilnius and Tallinn; the next one in Tallinn will be in June 2007.

Jaanipäev – Estonia's biggest annual night out takes place on 23 June, in celebration of the pagan Midsummer Eve. It's best experienced out in the country where huge bonfires flare for all-night partiers. If you're in the city, the Open Air Museum (p14) throws the best Jaanipäev.

Tallinn Old Town Days (www.vlp.ee) – Held in Tallinn's cinematic 14th-century quarters, this fest features lots of medieval amusement. It takes place in early June.

July

Beer Summer (www.ollesummer.ee; 1-day/ 5-day ticket around 100/300kr) – This extremely popular ale-guzzling, rock-music extravaganza happens under and around big tents near the Laulaväljak (Song Festival grounds) in early July.

August

Dance Festival (☎ 646 4704; www. saal.ee; per show ticket around 75kr) – Held the last two weeks in August, this highly recommended contemporary dance festival features troupes from all over Europe and the Baltics. Most performances are held at St Canutus Guild Hall (p17).

Brigitta Festival (www.filharmoonia. ee; per show ticket 150-250kr) – An excellent place to see some of Estonia's vibrant singing tradition, with choral, opera and classical concerts held at the Convent of St Brigitta (p20) over a five-day period. Book early; tickets sell out.

Levist Väljas (4, D2)
Inside this cellar bar, you'll find broken furniture, cheap booze and a refreshingly motley crew of punks, has-beens and anyone else who strays from the well-trodden tourist path. For some this is the quintessential Tallinn bar, for others it's an unpronounceable dive bar. Regardless, it's one possible choice when other bars close. ☎ 507 7372 ✉ Olevimägi 12 ☯ 3pm-3am Sun-Thu, 3pm-6am Fri-Sat

Scottish Club (4, D2)
With an extensive whisky menu and plenty of pub fare, this cosy bar and restaurant is a fine place to sit fireside with single malt (or haggis) in hand. A laid-back crowd meets on the manicured garden terrace in warmer weather. ☎ 641 1666 ✉ Uus 31 ☯ noon-11pm Mon-Sat

St Patrick's (4, D4)
One of the dozen or so of its ilk, this lively wooden

Dance the night away with the party crowd at Club Hollywood (p39)

bar has plenty of beer to go around and the comfy lounge in the adjoining room attracts a surprising number of Estonians. Expect plenty of tourists in the warmer months.

☎ 641 8173
✉ Suur-Karja tänav 8
☽ 11am-2am Sun-Thu, 11am-4am Fri-Sat

See and be seen at ice-cool Stereo

Stereo (4, C4)

White vinyl is the texture of choice at this painfully stylish club on the edge of Old Town. By night this sleek cube-like interior becomes the backdrop to DJs spinning a mix of global tunes to crowds of style mavens and their poseur friends. Love it or hate, Stereo is worth checking out – just don't forget your iPod.

☎ 631 0549 🖳 www.stereolounge.ee ✉ Harju tänav 6 ☽ 11am-1am Sun-Thu, 11am-3am Fri-Sat

Tapas & Vino (4, D4)

On a street packed with bars, this quaint tapas bar is a good place to slip away from the mayhem. There's an element of Andalusian charm to the place, with old stone walls, a slightly better-dressed crowd and tasty tapas selections to match the wines.

☎ 631 3232 ✉ Suur-Karja tänav 4 ☽ noon-midnight Sun-Thu, noon-2am Fri-Sat

Traveller's Pub & Club (3, D4)

A 20-minute walk from Old Town, the *Seiklusjutte Maalt ja Merelt*, as it's known in Estonian, is a true wanderer's hideaway, with maps and globes lending a cosy atmosphere to the lodge-like pub. During the summer, the peaceful courtyard is a fine detour for a drink.

☎ 601 0763
🖳 www.seiklusjutte.ee
✉ Tartu maantee 44
☽ 11am-midnight Sun-Thu, 11am-2am Fri-Sat

Vinoteek V & S (4, E2)

Just outside Old Town, this unpretentious wine bar is another enticing setting for a glass. Though once you get an eye of the fabulous views over Tallinn, you may end up staying for the bottle.

☎ 660 1818
✉ Mere puiestee 6e, 5th fl
☽ 2pm-midnight Sun-Thu, 2pm-1am Fri-Sat

DANCE CLUBS

Bon Bon (4, E2)
Set with enormous chandeliers and a portrait of Bacchus (the patron saint of decadence) overlooking the dance floor, Bon Bon is a recent favourite on the club circuit. Friday-night Brazilian fests are the recent big night event here.
☎ 661 6080 ✉ Mere puiestee 6e € 130-150kr ☾ 11pm-4am Fri-Sat

Club Hollywood (4, C4)
A multi-level setting inside Old Town, Club Hollywood is the one to draw the biggest crowds. Plenty of tourists and Tallinn's young party crowd mix it up. Wednesday's lively Ladies' Night is a perennial favourite.
☎ 627 4770 ☐ www.club-hollywood.ee ✉ Vana-Posti tänav 8 € 50-100kr ☾ 10pm-5am Wed-Sat

Moskva (4, C5)
This two-storey café and lounge hosts occasional dance parties, but any time is good to stop in for a cocktail and people-watching in the downstairs café. Visit Moskva's website to see what's on. See also p35.
☎ 640 4694 ☐ www.moskva.ee ✉ Vabaduse väljak 10 € free ☾ 9am-midnight Mon-Thu, 9am-4am Fri, 11am-4am Sat, 11am-midnight Sun

Privé (4, C5)
Tallinn's most elite club (note the deep red curtains and oxygen bar) gets rowdiest on Saturdays. High prices and good DJs attract a beautiful and foreign crowd. It's the only place in town where you can hit the oxygen tank, if you overdo it on the dance floor.
☎ 631 0545 ✉ Harju tänav 6 € 100-200kr ☾ 10pm-6am Wed-Sat

Terrarium (4, F1)
A more down-to-earth club experience is ensured here, with less attitude than in the posher Old Town clubs. Nevertheless, DJs still kick out the disco and the 20-something crowd laps it up. Don't overlook the outdoor terrace – anything can happen in the little pool there.
☎ 661 4721 ☐ www.terrarium.ee ✉ Sadama 6 € 50-100kr ☾ 10pm-4am Wed-Sat

GAY & LESBIAN VENUES

Angel (4, D4)
Tallinn's best gay club, Angel packs a festive, celebratory crowd. There's a balcony overlooking the dance floor, a men-only dark room and plenty of fine tunes pumping over the dance floor. Upstairs, the cosy restaurant serves plates till late in the night.
☎ 641 6880 ☐ www.clubangel.ee ✉ Sauna tänav 1 € 75-125kr ☾ 10pm-5am Wed-Sat

G-Punkt (4, C6)
Unsigned and hidden in an alley behind Pärnu maantee, this club recalls the secrecy of old Eastern European gay bars. Once inside, however, you'll join the cosy atmosphere, with a steady stream of regulars holding down the small dance floor till late most nights.
☎ 688 0747 ☐ www.baargpunkt.ee ✉ Pärnu maantee 23 € free ☾ 6pm-1am Sun-Tue & Thu; 6pm-4am Wed, Fri, Sat

X-Baar (4, D4)
The only place in Old Town flying the rainbow flag, X-Baar is Tallinn's oldest gay bar. The minuscule dance floor comes alive late at weekends. It's right next door to Angel – meaning you won't have to go far, if you're looking for something a little different.
☎ 692 9266 ✉ Sauna tänav 1 € free ☾ 2pm-1am

CINEMAS

To check out exactly what's showing in Tallinn, visit www.superkinod.ee. Films are shown in their original language and are subtitled in Estonian and Russian.

Coca-Cola Plaza (4, F3)
If you're in a bad way after a night out, or just need

a break from Old Town's medieval distractions, this super-modern 11-screen megaplex might be just the antidote. It shows the latest Hollywood releases in all their Digital Surround-Sound glory.
✉ Hobujaama tänav 5

Kino Sõprus (4, C4)
Set in a magnificent Stalin-era theatre, this art-house cinema has an excellent repertoire of European, local and independent productions. It's located on the southern fringe of Old Town.
☎ 644 1919 ✉ Vana-Posti 8

Kinomaja (4, D3)
A few blocks east of Raekoja plats, Kinomaja is another good art-house cinema, showing a selection of films from around the globe. At Kinomaja, which is run by Estonia's cinema union, you're more likely to find obscure prints that are not shown elsewhere.
☎ 646 4164 ✉ Uus tänav 3

PERFORMING ARTS

Tallinn has several theatre companies staging dramas (including translations of Western plays) in repertory from September until the end of May. Everything is in Estonian. A useful website for listings is www.concert.ee.

City Theatre (Linnateater) (4, C2)
The most-beloved theatre in town always stages something memorable. Watch for its summer plays on an outdoor stage.
☎ 665 0800
🖥 www.linnateater.ee
✉ Lai tänav 23

Estonia Drama Theatre (4, D4)
This long-standing favourite stages mainly classic plays and tends to avoid contemporary fare.
☎ 680 5555 ✉ Pärnu maantee 5

Estonia Theatre & Concert Hall (4, D4)
The premier venue for classical concerts, theatre and opera, this hall also hosts some big-name performers.
☎ 626 0215 (theatre),
☎ 614 7760 (concert hall), ☎ 683 1201 (opera)
🖥 www.concert.ee & www.opera.ee ✉ Estonia puiestee 4 🕑 box office noon-7pm Mon-Fri, noon-5pm Sat

Puppet Theatre (Nukuteater) (4, C3)
Not just for the kids, this lively theatre offers a range

The elegant façade of the Estonia Theatre & Concert Hall

BIG VENUES

International groups and top performers can be seen at various venues around town. **A. Le Coq Arena** (☎ 627 9940 ✉ Asula tänav 4c), located about 1.5km southwest of town, hosts big names in a large stadium setting. Closer to Old Town, **Estonia Concert Hall** (☎ 614 7760; www.concert.ee ✉ Estonia puiestee 4) also gets its share of well-knowns. From time to time, bands play in **Club Hollywood** (☎ 627 4770; www.club-hollywood.ee ✉ Vana-Posti tänav 8).

of colourful performances held throughout the year.
☎ 667 9555
🖳 www.nukuteater.ee
✉ Lai tänav 1

St Canutus Guild Hall
(4, D3)
This Old Town guild is now Tallinn's temple of modern dance, though it also hosts the rare classical dance performance. Regardless, it's hard to find a more atmospheric place to catch a show. St Canutus also hosts the annual dance festival held in August.
☎ 646 4704
🖳 www.saal.ee
✉ Pikk tänav 20

Von Krahl Theatre
(4, C3)
Synonymous with innovation, Von Krahl is highly regarded for its experimental and fringe productions. Although you may not understand much of an Estonian performance (even if you speak Estonian, as some critics gripe), this place is a part of history – it's the oldest private theatre in the country.
☎ 626 9090
🖳 www.vonkrahl.ee
✉ Rataskaevu tänav 10

LIVE MUSIC
Rock & Pop
Guitar Safari (4, D4)
On the southern fringe of Old Town, this basement bar draws a young, fairly alternative local crowd who come to hear some pretty rugged live shows. Guitar Safari is also one of the more consistent places to hear some music, with bands performing most nights of the week.
☎ 641 1607 ✉ Müürivahe tänav 22 € 25-50kr
🕑 noon-3am Mon-Fri, 2pm-3am Sat-Sun

Rock Café (3, E4)
Out past the bus station, this two-storey industrial space attracts some decent bands from Estonia and

abroad. Rock is the main event, though occasionally jazz, blues or funk make their appearance. Rock Café is housed in an old factory (hence the rugged façade), best reached by taxi or tram.
☎ 5695 8888
✉ Tartu maantee 80d
€ 35-100kr 🕑 9pm-4am Thu, 10pm-4am Fri-Sat
🚋 tram 2 or 4 to Lubja stop

Scotland Yard (4, E3)
This enormous Scottish-inspired pub packs crowds, with locals and foreigners mixing it up over Guinness and A. Le Coq. On weekends, there's usually a band (but never a cover), with a small dance floor that heats up as the night progresses.
☎ 653 5190 ✉ Mere puiestee 6e € free
🕑 noon-3am Mon-Fri, 2pm-3am Sat-Sun

Von Krahli Teater Baar (4, C3)
Attached to the theatre of the same name, the Von Krahli attracts a mixed, down-to-earth crowd, and it's one of our favourite bars in the city. Von Krahli hosts live bands and the

ostad napsi - toetad teatrit
buy a drink - support theatre

Sensible sales pitch at the Von Krahli Teater Baar

occasional fringe play, and it's a great place to meet some of Tallinn's more interesting locals.
☎ 626 9096 ✉ Rataskaevu tänav 12 € 50-75kr
☾ noon-1am Sun-Thu, noon-3am Fri-Sat

Classical Music

Chamber, organ, solo and other smaller-scale concerts are held in the Estonia Theatre's café (p40), in **Dome Church** (p11) and several halls around town, such as the **Town Hall** (p8) and the **Brotherhood of Blackheads** (p16), which has concerts almost nightly.

Holy Spirit Church (4, D3)

Just north of Raekoja plats, Holy Spirit Church (p15) hosts a classical music hour at least once a week inside its magnificent wood-carved interior. Chamber music is currently held on Monday at 6pm, though check with the tourist office for the latest times.
☎ 644 1487 ✉ Pühavaimu tänav 2 € 10kr

Linnahall (3, C2)

Housed in the rather dour 4200-seat monolith by the harbour, Linnahall hosts pop concerts, including the occasional big name, which will invariably be advertised months in advance.
☎ 641 1500 ⌨ www.linnahall.ee ✉ Mere puiestee 20

St Nicholas Church & Concert Hall (4, C4)

This atmospheric medieval church (p10) has incredible acoustics, making it an excellent place to catch one of the weekend concerts. Organ recitals and chamber music concerts take place here at 4pm on Saturday and Sunday.
☎ 631 4330
✉ Niguliste tänav 3
€ 35kr

SPORT

A. Le Coq Arena (3, B5)

About 1.5km southwest of town, this sparkling, newly refurbished arena is home to Tallinn's football team **Flora**, which is filled with Estonia's toughest, meanest players. If you have the chance, don't miss a lively match.
☎ 627 9940 ✉ Asula tänav 4c

Kalev Stadium (3, D4)

Basketball ranks as one of Estonia's most passionately watched games, and the best national tournaments are held in this stadium just south of town.
☎ 644 5171 ✉ Juhkentali tänav 12

THE CLASSICS OF ESTONIA

Tallinn's greatest home-grown composer, Arvo Pärt (b.1935), ranks among the world's most celebrated still active composers. Despite Estonia's isolation in the 1960s, Pärt's compositions were at the forefront of musical innovation as he experimented with serial and collage techniques. Two other famed Estonian composers are Veljo Tormis and Erkki-Sven Tüür, the latter being the youngest of the triad. Tüür, who splits his time between Tallinn and Hiiumaa island, cites the sea, earth and sky as elemental influences in his symphonic compositions (he also played in a rock band in the '70s). Today he continues to collaborate with some of the world's great performers.

Sleeping

Tallinn has a wide array of accommodation, from charming guesthouses to lavish four-star hotels. Old Town has the top picks, with plenty of atmospheric rooms set in beautifully refurbished medieval houses – though you'll pay a premium for it. During the summer, book far in advance.

ROOM RATES

The categories indicate the cost per night of a standard double room in high season.

Deluxe	over €200
Top End	€100–200
Midrange	€50–100
Budget	under €50

A grand entrance: door detail at the Three Sisters Hotel

DELUXE

Schlössle Hotel (4, D3)
This lovingly restored hotel features details from the original 17th-century building and its sumptuously decorated rooms are among the country's finest. If you make it out of your room, you'll enjoy the fireplace in the antique-laden great hall, the courtyard garden and the historically set cellar restaurant.
☎ 699 7700 ☐ www.schlossle-hotels.com
✉ Pühavaimu 13/15
✗ Stenhus

Three Sisters Hotel (4, D2)
Comprising three adjoining medieval houses, Three Sisters has spacious rooms with gorgeous details, including old-fashioned bathtubs in the rooms, original wooden beams, tiny balconies and canopy beds. You'll find plenty of romantic nooks to hide yourself away in on cold nights – the wine cellar, the fireside lounge and the lavish restaurant.
☎ 630 6300 ☐ www.threesistershotel.com
✉ Pikk tänav 71
✗ Restaurant Bordoo

TOP END

Baltic Hotel Imperial (4, C3)
This small luxury hotel has comfortable, modern rooms set in an old stone building with loads of character. Other pluses are the atmospheric lounge, the elegant St Michael Cheese Restaurant (with brown-robed servers, p32) and the adjoining indoor-outdoor pub.
☎ 627 4800 ☐ www.baltichotelgroup.ee
✉ Nunne 14
✗ St Michael Cheese Restaurant

Gloria Guesthouse (4, C4)
This small guesthouse has colourful rooms with lovely art deco details, and some beautiful antique furnishings (the owner is one of Estonia's biggest antique dealers). Artwork and old-fashioned wallpaper give a nostalgic feel to these charming rooms. Don't miss the exquisite restaurant (p30) and wine cellar (p36) downstairs.
☎ 644 6950 ☐ www.gloria.ee ✉ Müürivahe 2
✗ Gloria

Reval Hotel Olümpia (3, D3)
Built for the 1980 Moscow Olympics, this massive 26-storey hotel has modern, comfortable rooms with meticulous service, loads of amenities and enviable

Art nouveau style at a city guesthouse

views from the upper floors. If you stay here, don't miss the swimming pool and sauna on the top floor. The hotel lies about 700m south of Old Town.
☎ 631 5333 ⬛ www. revalhotels.com ✉ Liivalaia tänav 33 ✗ Café Boulevard

Sokos Hotel Viru (4, E4)
This high-rise hotel outside Old Town isn't much to look at, but the rooms inside are inviting, with hardwood floors, colourful furnishings and excellent views over Old Town.
☎ 680 9300 ⬛ www. viru.ee ✉ Viru väljak 4 ✗ Merineitsi

Taanilinna Hotell (4, D3)
Set in a converted 19th-century home, this four-star hotel has a range of wood-floored rooms, the best of which are spacious, tastefully furnished deluxe rooms with tubs in the bathrooms. The restaurant and wine cellar are equally atmospheric.
☎ 640 6700 ⬛ www. taanilinna.ee ✉ Uus tänav 6 ✗

MIDRANGE

Comfort Hotel Oru
(3, F2)
Set close to Kadriorg Park and Pirita tee, this modern hotel is a decent option for those who don't mind being outside the centre. Rooms are spacious but simple, with comfortable furnishings and big windows, giving a light, airy feel (some rooms have balconies or saunas).
☎ 603 3302 ⬛ www. oruhotel.ee ✉ Narva maantee 120b ⬛ 19, 29, 35 to Narva maantee ✗

Meriton Old Town Hotel
(4, D2)
This nicely located hotel has small but comfortable modern rooms, and it's hard to beat this price for en-suite quarters inside Old Town. Worth the extra are the six Bella Vita rooms, which are smarter and roomier (two have balconies).
☎ 614 1300 ⬛ www. meritonhotels.com ✉ Lai 49 ✗ Café Mademoiselle

Old House Guesthouse
(4, D2)
This cosy guesthouse with wood floors and tasteful furnishings offers warm and friendly hospitality in a superb neighbourhood. Their second location up the street (Uus tänav 26) functions more as a hostel, and has similarly charming features. Old House also rents 16 beautifully furnished apartments scattered through Old Town.
☎ 641 1464 ⬛ www. oldhouse.ee ✉ Uus tänav 22 ✗ African Kitchen (p29) is nearby

Pirita Top Spa Hotel
(3, F1)
On the seafront next to the Olympic Sailing Centre, the five-storey Pirita Top is Tallinn's premier spa hotel. Rooms are airy and bright, with parquet floors and a minimalist design, and some have sea-facing balconies. All guests enjoy free access to the pool and sauna, with spa services available.

APARTMENT RENTALS
Even if you're staying in Tallinn for just a few nights, you can find some great deals by booking an apartment. The following agencies all have websites where you can browse listings online. Apartments in Old Town start around €100 per night. Many even include free transport to and from the airport.
- **Cassandra Apartments** (3, D3; ☎ 630 9820; www.cassandra-apartments.com; Tartu maantee 18, 7th fl).
- **Erel International** (3, D3; ☎ 610 8780; www.erel. ee; Tartu maantee 14).
- **Rasastra** (4, E3; ☎ 661 6291; www.bedbreakfast. ee; Mere puiestee 4).
- **Red Group** (4, D4; ☎ 620 7877; www.redgroup.ee; Valli 4).

☎ 639 8600 🖳 www.topspa.ee ✉ Regati puiestee 1, Pirita 🍴

Reval Hotel Central (3, D3)
This large hotel remains one of the cheapest city-centre options. Bright, decent-sized rooms and friendly service come without a lick of pretence; and it's a short walk to Old Town.
☎ 633 9800 🖳 www.revalhotels.com ✉ Narva maantee 7 🍴

Valge Villa (3, A5)
This charming, family-run bed-and-breakfast has pleasant rooms with wooden floors, wood-panelled walls and good light. The owners will make you feel right at home. It's located 3km southwest of Old Town.
☎ 654 2302 🖳 www.white-villa.com ✉ Kännu tänav 26/2 🚋 2, 3, 4 to the Tedre stop

BUDGET

Euro Hostel (4, C3)
At Euro Hostel, it's all about the location. While the rooms are clean but nondescript and it has all the usual hostel amenities (kitchen use, dorm rooms, lockers), the setting just steps from Raekoja plats makes this a favourite. Book early to snag one of the private doubles.
☎ 644 7788 🖳 www.eurohostel.ee ✉ Nunne 2, 2nd fl 🍴 Kompressor (p31) is nearby

Hotell G9 (4, F4)
A few blocks from Old Town, Hotell G9 is a good choice for budget travellers who don't feel like bunking in a hostel. Rooms are simple and clean, with spartan furnishings and shared bathrooms down the hall.
☎ 626 7100 🖳 www.hotelg9.ee ✉ Gonsiori 9, 3rd fl

Old Town Backpackers Hostel (4, D3)
Young travellers flock to this recently opened hostel in Old Town. The space is small (just one big room of bunk beds), and if you're not up for the party atmosphere, look elsewhere. Bonuses: kitchen and sauna. In the summer, the staff arrange excursions out of town.
☎ 517 1337 🖳 www.balticbackpackers.com ✉ Uus tänav 14 🍴 African Kitchen (p29) is nearby

Tatari Hostel (4, D6)
Just outside Old Town, this hostel has clean rooms with tall ceilings on two renovated floors of an old building. It's a friendly place popular with a mix of travellers. Kitchen use and sauna available.
☎ 646 6287 🖳 www.tatarihostel.ee ✉ Tatari tänav 21b

Tapestry in the lobby of the Meriton Old Town Hotel

About Tallinn

Prior to 1991, Tallinn remained free of foreign rule during only one brief period (1919–40). Yet despite the waves of conquerors that have occupied their country over the last millennium, Estonians have clung tenaciously to their national identity.

Today, the proud capital has advanced by leaps and bounds beyond its Eastern bloc days. While Tallinn largely embraces its EU membership, things Estonian in nature still have a special status for most citizens, and the arts continue to flourish inside the capital.

HISTORY
Early Days
Stone Age settlements in Estonia date back to 8000 BC, although scholars equate the country's official beginnings with the arrival of Finno-Ugric tribes from the Urals around 2500 BC. There was probably an Estonian trading settlement here from around AD 800, with a wooden stronghold built atop Toompea hill in the 11th century.

The Estonians were a marked people when the pope called for a crusade against the nature-worshipping Baltic tribes. Answering the call, German knights and Danish soldiers attacked Estonia (and later each other) in the 13th century. The Danes, under King Waldemar II, conquered Toompea around 1219, and set up their own hilltop castle. A city grew from this settlement, bearing the name 'Tallinn' (from *Taani linn*, Estonian for 'Danish town').

After years of bloody uprising by ethnic Estonians in the mid-14th century, the Danes sold northern Estonia to the Teutonic Order. Tallinn, population 4000, became an important member of the Hanseatic League and a major trade link between Novgorod, Pskov and the West. German artisans and merchants propelled the economy until the brutal Livonian War (1558–83) decimated the country.

War & Peace
Russia, Sweden, Denmark and Poland battled for rulership. Despite a 29-week siege by Ivan the Terrible in 1570, Tallinn survived intact. The rest of the country, however, was in ruins. Sweden emerged the victor,

---

ESTONIAN ESOTERICA
- In the 1st century AD, the Roman historian Tacitus was the first to write of a people called *Aestii*.
- Estonia's first Song Festival was held in 1869, a major event in the National Awakening that ultimately led to independence.
- For centuries, Tallinn had deep German connections; until 1918, Tallinn's German name, Reval, coexisted with the local name.
- During Estonia's clamour for independence in 1991, Moscow ordered Soviet troops to quell the uprising. Commander Dzhokhar Dudayev, however, disobeyed orders and refused to fire upon the crowds. He later led Chechnya's own putsch towards independence, eventually becoming president of the separatist nation.

ushering in a long period of peace (1570–1710).

By the 18th century, Russia again had its sights on westward expansion. During the Great Northern War, in around 1710, Peter the Great attacked and conquered Tallinn along with the rest of Estonia. For the next 200 years, Estonia remained under Russian rule. This was bad news for the peasant class (exclusively native Estonians). Along with war, famine and plague, which killed tens of thousands in the early 1700s, the serfs continued to live in quasi-slavery until their emancipation in 1816.

Survey the horizon from the Old Town Wall (p18)

The National Awakening

The late 19th century was the dawn of the National Awakening, with significant steps towards nationhood. *Perno Postimees,* the first Estonian-language newspaper, appeared in 1857. It was the first to use the term 'Estonians' rather than *maarahvas* (country people). Numerous Estonian societies emerged, and Song Festivals created a sense of national pride. Estonia's rich folklore and poetry played a part, particularly works by Lydia Koidula (1834–86), which helped imprint upon the national consciousness the idea of 700 years of slavery. The movement reached its apotheosis in 1920, when Estonia, following a 13-month war with Russia, gained its independence.

WWII & Soviet Occupation

Independence ended in 1940, when during a secret German-Soviet pact, Estonia was handed over to Stalin. Tallinn suffered badly in WWII, with much destruction from Soviet bombers in 1944. After the war, the era of repression began as the Soviet Union seized power. Mass immigration from the east and gross industrialisation forever altered the city. Those who resisted the communist regime faced serious consequences. Thousands died in gulags; tens of thousands fled.

Independence

In the late '80s, Tallinn led the drive towards independence, and the regaining of nationhood in August 1991. Since then, the city has undergone much renovation, with a beautifully restored Old Town. Even before joining the EU in 2004, Estonia was experiencing explosive economic growth, led by entrepreneurs and IT-driven business. Today development projects are underway across the city.

ENVIRONMENT

Years of industrialisation beneath the Soviet yoke left behind environmental problems, though largely in the region east of Tallinn. Since independence, things have improved considerably. While the harbour around Tallinn is the most polluted part of the shoreline (from sewage overflows, storm water discharges and effluent from passenger ships), other parts of the bay are getting cleaner. Before becoming a member of the EU, Estonia joined international environmental conventions to protect the Baltic Sea.

Conservation continues to be an important topic in Estonia. Recent legislation such as 'the polluter pays', the emergence of environmental impact studies and the development of modern landfills demonstrate that Estonia is on the right track (meanwhile, the volume of pollution remains considerably below that of Western Europe).

GOVERNMENT & POLITICS

Tallinn is governed by a 63-member city council, a mayor and six deputy mayors. The city is divided into eight administrative districts, each managed by an elder along with the administrative council. Tallinn residents are fairly savvy about the latest happenings on the political front, perhaps owing to technological developments. Anyone can read, for instance, about the day's agenda in the *Riigikogu* (parliament), with access to most documents (the Internet portal www.erik.ee has links to all government websites).

In October 2005, Estonians participated in their first nationwide e-election, voting online. Government ministers have also taken to the Internet, creating paperless sessions of parliament, and thus saving time and money.

DID YOU KNOW?
- Population: 402,000
- Population growth: -1.6%
- Average temperature in July/February: 16/-3°C
- Longest and shortest day (summer/winter): 19/6hr
- Average gross wages per month in Tallinn/Estonia: 9249/7211kr
- Percentage of residents with a mobile phone/computer/car/dishwasher: 77/41/39/4
- Most common names given to boys/girls born in 2004: Nikita/Anastasija
- Number of foreign visitors per year: 3 million

ECONOMY

In economic terms, Estonia is often referred to as 'the little country that could, and did'. For the past four years, Estonia has experienced tremendous economic growth (averaging 6.1% per year, more than double that of the EU). Driving this economic engine is Tallinn, a city that has redefined itself as an entrepreneurial hotspot and a technological pioneer. Other factors in the country's economic success are its highly skilled and adaptable workforce (with rates of literacy and language skills well above the EU average), and the shrewd initial economic policies that helped create a stable currency.

Although most Tallinn residents view the future with hope, pensioners and older residents have often been left worse off by the radical changes brought about by Tallinn's new economy.

SOCIETY & CULTURE

Tallinn residents are known for their strong work ethic, and they're considered a versatile, technologically inclined crowd (you'll find more mobile phones per capita than in France, and the majority of residents do their banking online). Free weekends are spent out of town, hitting the beaches on warm summer days, hiking in the forest or simply relaxing at the country house (and requisite sauna).

In addition to a healthy respect for nature, Tallinn residents take great pride in their history, folklore and national song tradition (p19). Where else in the world will 250,000 fans pack a stadium to hear traditional folk singing?

Although relations aren't perfect between ethnic Estonians and Russians (who comprise 40% of Tallinn's population), things are improving, particularly as the youngest generation intermixes.

Tallinn pensioners take a break at Kadriorg Palace (p13)

Etiquette

Estonians are stereotyped as taciturn, reserved and even morose, which is only half true (usually between dark November and icy March, as one Estonian explained). Regardless, Estonians do tend towards modesty when it comes to vigorous public displays of affection (frowned upon), loud behaviour on buses and in public spaces (discouraged) and outward drunkenness (highly offensive – except on Jaanipäev, Midsummer's Night, when it's expected).

ARTS
Music

Estonia is widely known for its serious classical music tradition, and most notably its choirs. The Estonian Boys Choir and Tallinn Boys Choir are both highly acclaimed. Hortus Musicus, which was formed in 1972, is probably Estonia's best-known vocal ensemble, performing mainly music from the Middle Ages and the Renaissance.

The main Estonian composers of the 20th century all wrote music dear to the heart of the people, and remain popular today. Estonia's most celebrated composer is Tallinn-born Arvo Pärt (p42), the intense and reclusive master whose music many have misleadingly termed minimalist. One of Tallinn's rising composers is Erkki-Sven Tüür (b.1959), who takes inspiration from nature and the elements as experienced on his native Hiiumaa Island.

Literature

The long-time Tallinn resident Anton Hansen Tammsaare (1878–1940) is considered the greatest Estonian novelist for his *Tõde ja Õigus (Truth and Justice)*, written between 1926 and 1933. A five-volume saga of village and town life, it explores Estonian social, political and philosophical issues.

Eduard Vilde (1865–1933), who spent his last years in a house near Kadriorg (p13), was an influential novelist and playwright. In most of his novels and plays, Vilde looked with great irony at what he saw as Estonia's mad, blind rush to become part of Europe – themes some still find appropriate 75 years later. For Vilde, self-reliance was the truest form of independence.

Estonia's greatest contemporary writer is the novelist Jaan Kross (p27) who's won great acclaim for his historical novels, in which he manages to tackle Soviet-era subjects.

Theatre

Many of the country's theatre houses were built solely from donations by private citizens (sometimes collected door to door), which gives an indication of the role theatre has played in Estonian cultural life. The popularity of theatre is also evidenced in the high attendance of theatre-goers. Estonians visit the theatre almost as often as they go to the cinema, with 800,000 tickets sold annually.

Estonian theatre thrived during the country's independence days (1918–40). Experimentation became a hallmark of the theatrical repertoire then, with playwrights like Hugo Raudsepp (1883–1952) and the novelist Tammsaare creating widely acclaimed pieces for the stage.

The most original people on the theatre scene today are Jaanus Rohumaa, Katri Kaasik-Aaslav and Elmo Nüganen, all particularly sensitive directors with strong, personal styles who often work out of Tallinn's City Theatre.

Linnateater (p40), Tallinn's best loved theatre

Directory

ARRIVAL & DEPARTURE
Air
All flights arrive at **Tallinn Airport** (3, F5; Tallinna Lennujaam), located 3km southeast of Old Town on Tartu maantee. Frequent bus service links the airport with Old Town. Helicopter flights from Helsinki arrive at the **Copterline Tallinn Heliport** (3, C2) beside the Linnahall concert hall, about 500m north of Old Town. Despite an otherwise impressive safety record, Copterline had a fatal crash in 2005.

TALLINN AIRPORT Information
☎ 605 8888
🖳 www.tallinn-airport.ee

Airport Access
Bus 2 (15kr) runs every 20 to 30 minutes from terminals A and D to the Gonsiori bus stop near Kaubamaja (department store). From there it's another 400m to the edge of Old Town. The airport is just five bus stops to the centre. A taxi to or from the airport costs about 75kr.

COPTERLINE TALLINN HELIPORT Information
☎ 610 1818
🖳 www.copterline.ee

Heliport Access
There's no convenient bus service to the Heliport. If you'd rather not walk, Copterline can call a taxi, which should cost around 45kr from anywhere inside Old Town.

Bus
Buses to destinations within 40km or so of Tallinn depart from the platform next to the train station. You can get information and timetables from Harju Linnid (☎ 641 8218). Buses to all other destinations, including international ones, depart from the **Central Bus Station** (3, D4; Autobussijaam; ☎ 680 0900; www.bussireisid.ee; Lastekodu tänav 46), about 2km southeast of Old Town. Bus 17 or 23 (or tram 2 or 4) will take you there.

Train
Train service is limited in Estonia. All trains depart from **Central Station** (4, B2; Balti jaam; ☎ 615 6851; Toompuiestee 35) on the northwestern edge of Old Town, a short walk from Raekoja plats, or three stops on tram 1 or 2. The station has three ticket areas: for travel around Estonia visit the main hall; for international tickets go upstairs; and for electric trains *(elektrirong)* within the Tallinn area – including to Paldiski – visit the separate *elektriraudtee* ticket office (www.elektriraudtee.ee), next to the train platforms.

Boat
PORT OF TALLINN Information
Ferry Information
☎ 631 8550
Schedules Online
🖳 www.portoftallinn.com

Ferry Terminal Access
Tallinn's sea-passenger terminal is at the end of Sadama (3, D2), about 1km northeast of Old Town. Trams 1 and 2 and buses 3, 4 and 8 go to the Linnahall stop, five minutes' walk from terminals A, B and C. Terminal D is at the end of Lootsi tänav, better accessed from Ahtri tänav. A taxi between the centre and any terminal costs about 45kr.

Numerous ferries make the crossing between Helsinki and Tallinn each day. Passage on slow car ferries or speedy catamarans can be booked through **Tallink** (☎ 640 9808; www.tallink.ee), **Silja Line** (☎ 611 6661; www.silja.ee) or **Nordic Jet Line** (☎ 613 7000; www.njl.info), among other lines.

Travel Documents
PASSPORT
All arriving travellers need a passport, valid for three months beyond their planned stay.

VISA
Nationals of the US, Australia, New Zealand, Canada, the UK and other EU countries don't need a visa for stays of up to three months.

Customs & Duty Free
Non-EU residents can bring into Estonia duty-free two litres of wine, one litre of spirits and 200 cigarettes.

Left Luggage
Most hotels have luggage storage areas.
Tallinn Airport (3, F5; ☎ 605 8888; www.tallinn-airport.ee; 25kr for 24hr; 🕙 24hr)
Tallinn Central Bus Station (3, D4; ☎ 680 0900; www.bussireisid.ee; Lastekodu 46; 15-40kr for 24hr; 🕙 6.30am-10pm)

GETTING AROUND
Inside compact Old Tallinn, the best way to get around is on foot. Reaching destinations outside Old Town is best done via tram or bus. In this book, the nearest bus (🚌) or tram (🚋) line is noted after the appropriate symbol.

Travel Passes
Holders of the Tallinn Card (see Discounts, p53) can ride free on public transport. Travellers can also purchase a 24-hour ticket (40kr) or a three-day ticket (80kr), both available at kiosks. These tickets must be validated by the electronic device found on the second door of the vehicle, which will print the date and time on the ticket. Tallinn Card holders need only show their card.

Bus & Tram
Tallinn has an extensive bus and tram network, in operation from 6am until 11pm. An individual ticket for trams, buses and trolleybuses (which are electric buses) costs 10kr, available at any newspaper kiosk. You can also buy a ticket from the driver for 15kr. A book of ten tickets costs 80kr (also available at kiosks). After entering the vehicle, be sure to validate your ticket on the hole punch (or face a 600kr fine).

For transport maps and other service information get in touch with the **Tallinn Transport Department** (☎ 640 4618; www.tallinn.ee).

Taxi
Taxis are plentiful in Tallinn. Journeys are metered and should cost around 7kr per km. However, if you merely hail one on the street, there's a fair chance you'll be overcharged. To save yourself the trouble, order a taxi by phone. Operators speak English; they'll tell you the car number (licence plate) and estimated arrival time (usually five to ten minutes).
A few options:
Kiisu Takso (☎ 655 0777)
Krooni Takso (☎ 638 1111)
Linnatakso (☎ 644 2442) They also have vehicles for disabled travellers.

Car & Motorcycle
On a short trip to Tallinn, you're unlikely to need your own wheels. However, if you do need to hire a vehicle, you could try **Tulikarent** (☎ 612 0012; www.tulikatasko.ee; Tihase 34) southwest of Old Town or **R-Rent** (☎ 605 8929; www.rrent.ee), **Hertz** (☎ 605 8953; www.hertz.ee) or **Budget** (☎ 605 8600; www.budget.ee) at the airport.

PRACTICALITIES
Climate & When to Go
The months of June to September are the best time to visit Tallinn. This is when the weather is warmest, and Tallinn is at its liveliest, with festivals packing the summer calendar. Unfortunately, this is also when

the tourist hordes invade Tallinn, creating a scarcity of accommodation in the city. July and August, while the warmest months, also get the most rainfall, so don't forget to bring wet weather gear. To experience Tallinn without the masses, plan a trip between October and May. In winter, the cobbled streets lie glazed in snow, though you'll have to contend with temperatures that rarely rise above 4°C from November to March.

Disabled Travellers

With its cobbled streets, rickety pavements and old buildings, Tallinn is not user-friendly for travellers with disabilities. The **Social Rehabilitation Centre** (☎ 658 6355; srk@ngonet.ee; Männiku tee 92) gives advice to travellers with disabilities.

Discounts

Most children under 12 pay a reduced price at museums and other sights as well as on public transport. Under our listings, we've given adult prices followed by the reduced charges for children and for students possessing an ISIC card.

THE TALLINN CARD

This discount card gives you free or discounted entry to many of the city's sights, discount shopping and free use of public transport. Prices for one-/two-/three-day cards are 350/400/450kr (125/150/175kr for children) and include a free 2½-hour city tour. Cards are sold at tourist information centres, hotels and travel agencies. Further details are available on www.tallinn.ee/tallinncard.

STUDENT & YOUTH CARDS

An International Student Identity Card (ISIC) will give discounted admission to most museums and sights as well as discounted fares on public transport.

Electricity

Voltage	220V
Frequency	50Hz
Cycle	AC
Plugs	two round pins

Embassies

Canada (4, B4; ☎ 627 3311; tallinn @canada.ee; Toomkooli tänav 13)
Finland (4, B4; ☎ 610 3200; www. finland.ee; Kohtu tänav 4)
Ireland (4, D4; ☎ 681 1888; embassytallinn@eircom.net; Vene tänav 2)
Lithuania (4, D3; ☎ 631 4030; www.hot. ee/lietambasada; Uus tänav 15)
Russia (4, C3; ☎ 646 4175; www.estonia. mid.ru; Lai tänav 18)
UK (4, A5; ☎ 667 4700; www. britishembassy.ee; Wismari tänav 6)
USA (4, E6; ☎ 668 8100; www.usemb.ee; Kentmanni tänav 20)

Emergencies

In comparison to Rome, Paris or London, Tallinn is a fairly safe city; but don't get complacent. Pickpocketing and petty theft (bag-snatching) are a risk here – particularly in the busy summer. Keep an eye out when you're exploring those enchanting old quarters. Late at night, there are occasional muggings on the street. Always be mindful of your surroundings, and be sensible about where you go and with whom you go. If you're driving, don't leave anything of value in your car after you park it.
Ambulance ☎ 112
Fire ☎ 112
First-Aid Hotline ☎ 110; English-language advice on treatment, hospitals and pharmacies

Police ☎ 110; To report a crime contact the central police station (☎ 612 4200; Pärnu maantee 11)

Fitness
SAUNAS

Locals attribute all kinds of health benefits to a good old-fashioned sweat-out, and a trip to Estonia just won't be complete until you've paid a visit to the sauna. You won't have to look far: nearly every place listed in Sleeping (pp43–45) has one. Other saunas you might try:

Beer House (4, C4; ☎ 627 6520; www. beerhouse.ee; Dunkri 5; per hour 300-600kr; ☺ 10am-midnight Sun-Thu, 10am-2am Fri-Sat) Two private saunas for rent (the larger has a Jacuzzi) in this large beer hall.

Kalma Saun (4, B1; ☎ 627 1811; Vana-Kalamaja 9a; per person 60-90kr; ☺ 10am-11pm) Tallinn's oldest public bath with the feel of an old-fashioned Russian-style *banya* (bath house).

SPAS, HEALTH CLUBS & POOLS

Body Zone (3, F1; ☎ 630 0940; www. bodyzone.ee; Merivälja tee 5; one-day pass 300-400kr; ☺ 7am-10pm Mon-Fri, 9am-6pm Sat, 11am-8pm Sun) Pool, squash courts, several rooms full of machines and weights, and a wide variety of classes (aerobics, yoga, cardio dance, spinning), plus a full-service spa.

Club 26 (3, D3; ☎ 631 5585; www. revalhotels.com; Reval Hotel Olümpia, Liivalaia tänav 33, 26th fl; per visit 60-130kr; ☺ 6.30am-11pm Mon-Fri, 7:30am-11pm Sat-Sun) This small health club has a gym, sauna and 16m swimming pool with superb views over the city. Good choice for a workout without breaking the bank.

Kalev (4, E3; ☎ 644 2286; Aia tänav 18; per visit 50-70kr; ☺ 7am-9.30pm Mon-Fri, 9am-8.45pm Sat-Sun) For serious swimming in an indoor pool of Olympic proportions. Sauna is also available.

Tallinn Sports Hall (3, D4; ☎ 646 6346; Herne tänav 30; per visit 25-75kr; ☺ 7am-9.30pm Mon-Fri, 9am-8.45pm Sat-Sun) Huge indoor running track, top-notch gym and the all-essential sauna.

Top Spa (3, F1; ☎ 639 8718; www. topspa.ee; Regati puiestee 1; swimming pool per person 60-90kr; ☺ spa 8am-6pm Mon-Fri, 8am-3pm Sat; swimming pool 6.30am-10pm Mon-Fri, 8am-10pm Sat-Sun) Inside the Hotel Pirita (p44), this spa offers a number of pampering options (massages, salt chamber, solarium, pedicures, etc). The adjoining health club has a gym where you can work out, catch a yoga or aerobics class or swim the 25m, six-lane pool.

Gay & Lesbian Travellers

Homosexuality was legalised here in 1992, and although there have been some strides in gay rights in recent years, most gay Estonians remain in the closet. Although gay-bashing and overt discrimination are rare inside the laid-back capital, most gays feel that being out would be detrimental to a career. Estonia's key gay organisation is the **Estonian Gay League** (gayliit@ hotmail.com). **Estonian Gay Planet** (www. gay.ee) lists party venues in Estonian only. The **Gay and Lesbian Info Centre** (3, D3; ☎ 645 4545; www.pride.gay.ee; Tartu maantee 29, Tallinn) is a good source of info.

Health
PRECAUTIONS

Food preparation standards are generally high, and the tap water is drinkable in Tallinn, though many Estonians prefer the taste of bottled water. Although balmy weather is rare in Tallinn, the long summer days could leave you with pretty serious sunburn. More of an issue are icy cold winds and rain; bring a reliable jacket, even during the summer. If you come in winter, be mindful of sword-length icicles, which plummet onto the pavements during sudden thaws.

MEDICAL SERVICES

Travel insurance is advisable to cover any medical treatment you may need while in Tallinn. Health care is emerging from the grim Soviet-era days, though underfunded state hospitals are still prevalent. For emergencies, visit **Tallinn Central Hospital** (3, C4; ☎ 620 7015; Ravi tänav 18), which provides a full range of services, a polyclinic and a 24-hour emergency department; they're used to foreigners dropping in.

DENTAL SERVICES

If you chip a tooth or require emergency treatment, head to the state-run **Tallinna Hambapolikliinik** (4, A4; ☎ 611 9230; Toompuiestee tänav 4).

PHARMACIES

The following pharmacies are well stocked and have long opening hours. You'll find English-speaking staff here too.
Aia Apteek (4, E3; ☎ 627 3607; Aia tänav 10; ☼ 8.30am-midnight)
Tallinna Linnaapteek (4, D4; ☎ 644 0244; Pärnu maantee 10; ☼ 24hr)

Holidays

New Year's Day	1 January
Independence Day Anniversary of 1918 declaration	24 February
Good Friday – Easter Monday is also commonly taken as a holiday	March/April
Spring Day	1 May
Võidupüha Victory	23 June
Jaanipäev (St John's Day; Midsummer's Night)	eve of 23 June to 24 June
Day of Restoration of Independence (1991)	20 August
Christmas Day (Jõulud)	25 December
Boxing Day	26 December

Metric System

Estonia uses the metric system. Commas are used in decimal numbers and full stops to indicate thousands.

Internet

Wireless Internet access (WiFi) is extremely widespread in Estonia. You'll find over 225 hot spots in Tallinn, and in many places connection is free (see wwww.wifi.ee for a complete list). The only adjustment you may have to make is to set your out-going mail server (SMTP) to connect to a local host like mail.hot.ee. If you're not packing a laptop, you'll find numerous Internet cafés in Tallinn (charging around 30-60kr per hour).

INTERNET SERVICE PROVIDERS

Tele2 (⌨ www.tele2.ee) is one of the major Internet service providers in the country. To access it, simply set your modem to dial 901 9777.

INTERNET CAFÉS

Estonian National Library (4, B6; ☎ 630 7381; Tõnismägi 2, room C-2118; per hr 40kr; ☼ 10am-8pm Mon-Fri, noon-7pm Sat Sep-Jun; noon-7pm Mon-Fri Jul-Aug)
Matrix Club (3, D3; ☎ 641 9442; Tartu maantee 31; per hr 20kr; ☼ 24hr)
Reval Café (4, E3; ☎ 627 1229; Aia tänav 3; per hr 40kr; ☼ 9am-9pm)

USEFUL WEBSITES

The Lonely Planet website (www.lonelyplanet.com) offers a speedy link to many of Tallinn's websites. Others to try include:
In Your Pocket (www.inyourpocket.com)
Tallinn Tourist Office (www.tourism.tallinn.com)

Lost Property

If you leave something on a bus or tram contact the **City Transport Department**

(4, C5; ☎ 640 4618; tta@tallinnlv.ee; Vabaduse väljak 10).

Money
CURRENCY
Estonia's currency is the kroon (pronounced 'krohn'), which is pegged to the euro. The kroon comes in two, five, 10, 25, 50, 100 and 500kr notes. One kroon is divided into 100 sents (cents), and there are coins of five, 10, 20 and 50 sents, as well as one- and five-kroon coins. Estonia has a fair chance of adopting the euro by 2007.

TRAVELLERS CHEQUES
American Express and Thomas Cook are the most widely accepted travellers cheques, exchangeable at most banks and exchange offices. The commission at most banks is around 4.5%.

CREDIT CARDS
Visa and Mastercard are the most widely accepted credit cards in Tallinn.
For 24-hour card cancellations or assistance:
American Express ☎ 358 9613 20400 (Finland)
Diners Club ☎ 358 800 95 555 (Finland)
MasterCard ☎ 08001 156 234 (Finland)
Visa ☎ 800 12001

ATMS
ATMs are widespread in the city. You won't have to look far in Old Town.

CHANGING MONEY
Currency exchange is available at all transport terminals, inside banks, major hotels and the post office. Among the numerous exchange bureaus, **Tavid** (4, E3; ☎ 627 9900; Aia tänav 5; ☾ 24hr) often has the best rates.

For current exchange rates see www.xe.com.

Australia	A$1	10EEK
Canada	C$1	12EEK
Euro zone	€1	16EEK
Japan	¥100	11EEK
New Zealand	NZ$1	9EEK
Russia	R100	47EEK
UK	£1	23EEK
USA	US$1	13EEK

Newspapers & Magazines
For news, the best English-language weekly is *The Baltic Times*. The bi-monthly *City Paper* is a glossy magazine with in-depth articles and sometimes quirky features.

Opening Hours
Banks ☾ 9am-4pm Mon-Fri
Bars ☾ noon-midnight Sun-Thu, noon-2am Fri & Sat
Cafés ☾ 9am-10pm
Nightclubs ☾ 10pm-4am Thu-Sat
Post Offices ☾ 9am-6pm Mon-Fri, 9am-3pm Sat
Restaurants ☾ noon-11pm
Shops ☾ 10am-6pm Mon-Fri, 10am-3pm Sat
Supermarkets ☾ 9am-10pm

Photography & Video
The most convenient place in Old Town for film purchase and development is **Filmari** (☎ 644 3023; www.fuji.ee; Suur-Karja tänav 9; ☾ 9am-7pm Mon-Fri, 10am-5pm Sat). Estonia uses the PAL video system (the same as elsewhere in Europe, except France).

Post
Mail service in and out of Estonia is highly efficient. Most letters or postcards take about one or two days within Estonia, three or four days to Western Europe and about a week to North America and other destinations outside Europe. You can buy stamps from any kiosk and then deposit the postcard or letter in any orange post box around town.

POSTAL RATES
Destination	Weight	Cost (kr)
UK & Western Europe	20/50g	6.50/10
USA & Canda	20/50g	8/13.50

Radio

Radio 2 (101.6) and Sky Plus (95.4) are the two most popular radio stations among Estonia's pop and Euro-disco lovers.

Telephone

Payphones are scattered around the city, most locals have a mobile phone. Estonian payphones work on a phonecard system.

PHONECARDS

You can purchase phonecards, in denominations of 30, 50 or 100kr, from any kiosk. As elsewhere in the world, calling mobile phone numbers burns through a phonecard much faster than calling a land line.

MOBILE PHONES

Mobile phones that work on the GSM mobile network in Europe and the UK will work here. To avoid the high roaming charges, you can get a starter kit (around 150kr), which will give you an Estonian number, a SIM card that you pop into your phone and around 100kr of talk time (incoming calls are free with most providers). You can buy scratch-off cards for more minutes as you need them. SIM cards and starter kits are available from post offices, kiosks and mobile phone shops.

COUNTRY & CITY CODES

Estonia phased out all city codes in 2004. If you're calling another city, just dial the number as listed. All Estonian land lines have seven digits; mobile phones have seven or eight digits and begin with a 5.

USEFUL PHONE NUMBERS

Information (addresses, transport, events in English)	☎ 626 1111
Operator	☎ 16115
Reverse-Charge (collect)	☎ 16116

Television

In addition to viewing Estonia's three channels (TV3, Kanal 2 and the public, commercial-free network ETV), Tallinn visitors can pick up three Finnish channels. Most hotels, midrange and higher, have cable TV (with around 100 channels).

Time

Standard Time is two hours ahead of GMT/UTC. Daylight-saving time is practised from the last Sunday in March to the last Sunday in October. At this time it's GMT +3.

Tipping

It's fairly common to tip restaurant servers 10%. Tipping taxi drivers is not usual.

Tourist Information

Central Tourist Office (4, C4; ☎ 645 7777; www.tourism.tallinn.com; Niguliste tänav 2; 🕑 9am-8pm Mon-Fri, 10am-6pm Sat & Sun May-Aug; 9am-6pm Mon-Fri, 10am-6pm Sat & Sun Sep; 9am-5pm Mon-Fri, 10am-3pm Sat & Sun Oct-Apr) is particularly helpful for obtaining the latest information about what's happening around town. They have loads of brochures as a whole and can book accommodation for you.

Port tourist office (3, D2; ☎ /fax 631 8321; Terminal A, Tallinn harbour; 🕑 8am-4.30pm)

MOBILE SERVICES

Express Hotline (☎ 1182; www.1182.ee; per min 2.60kr) Accessible only from mobile phones, this English-speaking source has telephone numbers, transport schedules, theatre listings, etc. The website is also useful – and free.

Infoline (☎ 626 1111) Provides free, useful information in English 24 hours a day.

Women Travellers

Women are not likely to receive aggressive attention from men in Tallinn, although unaccompanied women may want to avoid a few of the sleazier bars and beer cellars.

LANGUAGE

Like Finnish, Estonian belongs to the Finnish-Ugric family of languages and is fiendishly difficult to learn. Luckily, most Estonians in Tallinn speak at least some English; many speak it fluently. You're unlikely to pick up more than a smattering of Estonian in a short visit, but knowing a few basic words and phrases will go down well with the people you meet. For trivia buffs, Estonian boasts the word with the most consecutively repeated vowel: *jäääär*, which means 'edge of ice'.

PRONUNCIATION

Estonian lacks a few letters of the English alphabet but has some extra ones of its own.

The alphabet is as follows: a b d e f g h i j k l m n o p r s š z ž t u v õ ä ö ü.

When pronouncing a word, the emphasis is always on the first syllable. Letters are generally pronounced as in English. The following outlines some pronunciations that are specific to Estonian.

a	as the 'u' in 'cut'
b	similar to English 'p'
g	similar to English 'k'
j	as the 'y' in 'yes'
š	as 'sh'
ž	as the 's' in 'pleasure'
õ	somewhere between the 'e' in 'bed' and the 'u' in 'fur'
ä	as the 'a' in 'cat'
ö	as the 'u' in 'fur' but with rounded lips
ü	as a short 'you'
ai	as the 'i' in 'pine'
ei	as in 'vein'
oo	as the 'a' in 'water'
uu	as the 'oo' in 'boot'
öö	as the 'u' in 'fur'

SOCIAL

Hello.	Tere.
Goodbye.	Head aega.
Yes/No.	Jah/Ei.
Please.	Palun.
Thank you.	Tänan.
You're welcome.	Palun.
Excuse me.	Vabandage.
Sorry. (Forgive me)	Vabandage.
Do you speak English?	Kas te räägite inglise keelt?
I don't speak Estonian	Ma ci räägi eesti kelt.
I don't understand.	Ma ei saa aru.

PRACTICAL

When does the ... leave?	Mis kell läheb ...?
bus	buss
boat	paat
train	rong
tram	trammiga
taxi	takso
airport	lennujaam
bus station	bussijaam
port	sadam
railway station	raudteejaam
stop (eg bus stop)	peatus

arrival/arrival time	saabub/ saabumine
departure/departure time	väljub/väljumine

I'd like a ... ticket.	Palun ... pilet.
one-way	üks
return	edasi-tagasi

Where is ...?	Kus on ...?
Go straight ahead.	Otse.
Turn left/right.	Vasakule/Paremale.

I'm looking for ...	Kus on ...?
a bank	pank
a chemist	apteek
a currency exchange	valuutavahetus
a department store	kaubamaja
a hospital	haigla
a hotel	hotell
the market	turg
a post office	post kontor

a public toilet	tualett	January	jaanuar
the tourist office	turismibüroo	February	veebruar
		March	märts
What time does it	Mis kell see	April	aprill
open/close?	avatakse/	May	mai
	suletakse?	June	juuni
		July	juuli
I'd like a ...	Ma tahaksin	August	august
	... tuba.	September	september
single room	ühe voodiga	October	oktoober
double room	kahe voodiga	November	november
room with a		December	detsember
bathroom	vannitoaga		
Are there any	Kas teil on	1	üks
cheaper	odavamaid	2	kaks
rooms?	tube?	3	kolm
		4	neli
breakfast	hommikusöök	5	viis
lunch	lõuna	6	kuus
dinner	õhtusöök	7	seitse
The bill, please.	Palun arve.	8	kaheksa
		9	üheksa
I'd like to	Ma tahaksin	10	kümme
buy ...	osta ...	20	kakskümmend
How much	Kui palju see	100	sada
is it?	maksab?	1000	tuhat
Can I pay by	Kas teil saab		
credit card?	maksta	**EMERGENCIES**	
	krediitkaardiga?	Help!	Appi!
		I'm ill.	Ma olen haige.
What time is it?	Mis kell on?	I'm lost.	Ma olen eksinud.
today	täna	Go away!	Minge ära!
tomorrow	homme		
yesterday	eile	Call ...!	Kutsuge ...!
morning	hommik	a doctor	arst
afternoon	pärastlõuna	an ambulance	kiirabi
evening	õhtu	the police	politsei
day	päev		
night	öö	**SIGNS**	
		entrance	sissepääs
Monday	esmaspäev	exit	väljapääs
Tuesday	teisipäev	open	avatud/lahti
Wednesday	kolmapäev	closed	suletud/kinni
Thursday	neljapäev	no smoking	mitte suitsetada
Friday	reede	toilet	WC
Saturday	laupäev	women	meestele
Sunday	pühapäev	men	naistele

Index

See also separate indexes for Eating (p62), Sleeping (p62), Shopping (p62) and Sights with map references (p63).

EATING

SLEEPING

SHOPPING

SIGHTS

FEATURES

Villa Thai	*Eating*
Estonia Theatre	*Entertainment*
Tapas & Vino	*Drinking*
Café Peterson	*Café*
City Museum	*Highlights*
Bogapott	*Shopping*
Tallinn Art Hall	*Sights/Activities*
Reval Hotel Central	*Sleeping*
Paldiski	*Trips & Tours*

AREAS

	Beach, Desert
	Building
	Land
	Mall
	Other Area
	Park/Cemetery
	Sports
	Urban

HYDROGRAPHY

	River, Creek
	Intermittent River
	Canal
	Swamp
	Water

BOUNDARIES

	International
	Ancient Wall

ROUTES

	Tollway
	Freeway
	Primary Road
	Secondary Road
	Tertiary Road
	Lane
	Under Construction
	One-Way Street
	Unsealed Road
	Mall/Steps
	Tunnel
	Walking Path
	Walking Trail/Track
	Pedestrian Overpass
	Walking Tour

TRANSPORT

	Airport, Airfield
	Bus Route
	Cycling, Bicycle Path
	Ferry
	General Transport
	Metro
	Monorail
	Rail
	Taxi Rank
	Tram

SYMBOLS

	Bank, ATM
	Beach
	Buddhist
	Castle, Fortress
	Christian
	Embassy, Consulate
	Hospital, Clinic
	Information
	Internet Access
	Islamic
	Jewish
	Lighthouse
	Lookout
	Monument
	Mountain, Volcano
	National Park
	Parking Area
	Petrol Station
	Picnic Area
	Point of Interest
	Police Station
	Post Office
	Ruin
	Swimming Pool
	Telephone
	Toilet
	Zoo, Bird Sanctuary